All These Presences

# All These Presences

Edited by
Jean Kent, David Musgrave
& Carolyn Rickett

Puncher & Wattmann

First published in 2016, revised 2016

Published by Puncher and Wattmann
PO Box 441
Glebe NSW 2037

http://www.puncherandwattmann.com

puncherandwattmann@bigpond.com

National Library of Australia
Cataloguing-in-Publication entry:

Jean Kent, David Musgrave & Carolyn Rickett (eds.)

All These Presences

ISBN 9781922186928

I. Title.

A821.3

Cover design by Chloe Lwin, 'That Design' Intern

Printed by McPhersons Printing Group

*For Judith Beveridge*

Judith Beveridge is a distinguished poet of rare compassion and intelligence.

As a practicing writer she may often sit in her garage with headphones over her ears to block out the clamour of the daily world. With dedication and diligence, there she summons presences and voices and creates another, more intensely real world to haunt and delight her readers. From Sydney to India, from mangrove mud flats to egg shells which could be temples for snails, she brings us gravitas and grace: crafted visions, 'stilled to perfection'.

Alone— on the days when creativity is possible— this is her vocation. On other days, though, she also goes out into the everyday world and teaches students, mentors other poets, judges competitions, edits anthologies, shares the triumphs and trials of her fellow writers, celebrates the possibilities of poetry, and selflessly encourages other readers and writers.

In her life as a poet, as well as in her poetry, she is an inspiration.

Judith has had a long association with Avondale College of Higher Education, both as a teacher of creative writing and as co-editor of the four anthologies which preceded *All These Presences*. With their thoughtful assembling of student work alongside contributions by established Australian and international poets, these anthologies are beautifully concrete testimonies to Judith's belief in the power of poetry to connect people, and her desire to pass on her love of poetry to others.

We dedicate this new volume to her, in gratitude, not only for the extraordinary gift of her own poetry, but also for her generous fostering of our poetic community.

*— Jean Kent, Dr David Musgrave & Dr Carolyn Rickett*
*July, 2016*

# Contents

## All these presences!

The power of poetry lies in the artistic authority it assumes, an authority that is at once personal, communal and lyrical. It attests to the legitimacy of human experience and personal testimony, validating our thirst to co-create, to witness and memorialise. If poetry must be 'pleasurably right' and 'compellingly wise' it must also be provocative in purpose; it must re-engineer our perspectives to effect 'a re-tuning of the world itself'! [Heaney, Nobel Lecture 1995]. This 're-tuning' responds to the intersecting 'presences' within a poem! Poetry, then, connotes a prevailing presence or presences, and *all these presences* become a conduit for meditation. In that meditation we hold vigil with our deepest selves and our sharpest senses, and we rest and play and feel and learn in a community that is connected only through the artefact of the poem itself!

This anthology is dedicated to that sacred cord that binds us, the tangible and intangible connections by which through poetry we belong to each other. *All These Presences* enacts a witness to that bond articulated here through the collaboration of students, teachers and eminent poets of our time.

It is a fitting tribute to the power of intuition and collaboration and the mystique of all these/those presences that shape our best selves!

My heartiest congratulations to Dr Carolyn Rickett, Jean Kent, Dr David Musgrave, Judith Beveridge and Margaret House for their leadership and management of the anthology project and to all students for your creative participation in this worthy project. My very special thanks to the established poets for your time and investment in inspiring and supporting our journey. Avondale is grateful for, and privileged by, your collaboration.

—Professor Jane Fernandez
Vice President (Quality & Strategy)
Avondale College of Higher Education

*I have never started a poem yet whose end I knew.*

*Writing a poem is discovering.*

— Robert Frost

## Knots

I reach inside,
grasping the knots

Those that strangle
or even tug a little.

Attempts are clumsy
when I yank them apart,
to make sense of the frayed strands.

A letter
              for each nonsensical thread
it all becomes tangible
and I don't just feel it.

Calm immobility on a white page,
frozen and comprehendible.

I push the ropes back where I found them
in dark spaces now easier to visit,
disentangled.

HAYLEY ANTOLOS

## The Sound Review

*for my grandmother*

We turn in circles,
to strings spinning with us
from the crackling record.

We pull her faded skirts to our collarbones
amused by movement alone,
in awe of ourselves

because her eyes are mirrors
for our childish pride–
exclamations of wonder
and admiration.

Our steps lose hesitation
under her loving review

And we accept it all,
because words become truth
in her voice

## My Mother's Hands

*in loving memory of Kerrie J. Armstrong 27/07/1957 – 25/04/2014*

When I look at my hands
from time to time
I think of hers,
my Mother's hand's

Pale and lightly freckled,
blue veins bulged
snaking from her wrists

As she spoke her hands would
frantically wave about
filled with passion, as though
words could only say so much

Her nails, kept short
stained by bleach and OMO,
in soapy dishwater
together we pruned our hands

They were not pretty,
but wrinkled and patchy –
they were my mother's hands
beautiful to me

## An Autumn Dip

toes curled
clinging to craggy rocks
light warps in twisted waves,
I leap

salted champagne
crashing, spilling
spume seeps
through sieve of stone

cave's mouth
breathes
as waves crash in
and tide withdraws

tight skin
lips slapped by spindrift spray
salted and wrinkled.

# Callala Dreaming

*here now*
choreographed quartet of pelicans
skim-silent, stately squadron formation
dark against deepening sky
white noise
sea breathing
*later when*
silence shaken, broken
startling rhythmic thudding
frustrated fury-violent screams
policemen gather
white van
let me out
*there then*
sea breathing white noise
crisp colour clarity
the senses ache
flame-red weed like broken bodies
sinking silence
reset
knit and mend

## Herons at Dusk

This is the time of day when the light runs down the sky
like bluing and meets the bay, when whipbirds set acoustic
flares along the trees, when I'll stand and listen to the yachts,
a sound as if cutlery were being replenished on tabletops;

but most of all when I love to watch the herons step along
the shore, how like tai chi performers they will step deftly,
easily into constantly reconfigured stances. I can see one
down by the mangroves now, moving and then redoing

each step as though it has become fastidious about how
to present the curve of its neck, a punctilio it must get right
before it will allow itself to stand twinned to its reflection.
Near the pier another heron is holding its bill over the reeds

as purposeful as a seiner with a marlinespike, before it
jabs then returns to its wire-drawn stance, as if all it must
achieve now is to lift and pull itself into the distance
like sail twine. When the herons quietly step they make

even the stilts' and avocets' neat stabs along the sand
seem like slapstick; they make the routines of all who fish
along the shore at dusk seem over-weighted and vaudevillian.
And look! how they stand — at last — stilled to perfection.

## Naming Roses

This one is called *Grandchild*, this *Happy Days*,
this one is *Soliloquy*, this is *Crosby*
and this one—*Maria Callas.*
Blossoms of light, they stand idle and blessed
like luminaries. Soon she will hold
the spent petals, the public scents—
but for a moment she pauses,

lifts her head—as if some perfume
takes her back through open gardens and doors—
to a woman holding roses close to her face,

a bright red bunch given to her
with words and sweet breath,
with promises and days to order
with wine and the music of venues and events.
She hears the music she would love to sing to
as she pauses over the roses, and her life

is no longer here in this chill afternoon garden,
but is a fragrance that travels incognito
in her hands: singular and rare.
She intones the idol in each unhurried petal
and listens to the ways some days are shaped:
*Rendezvous*, *Soirée*, *Tête-à-Tête*

and all the paths are full that fill
the intimate fragrance of her life:
each rose a door swinging open
as she strays then leaves, room by room, for the night—
whispering *Cheer*, *Fiesta*, *Camaraderie*
as if she knew she would never be more alone than she wanted;

past *Stage Door*, *Recital*, *Double Ovation*—
as if roses would always be giving their lives
and their small performances;

as if she would always
be bending to roses on calm clear nights,
as if each were the stairway out of a stuffy house.

And by bending
to the pure fragrance of her life
she could sing any song she wanted, any way she chose.

## The second word of infinity's other name overheard by a young woman crossing the intersection of Maldonado and Paraguay

You grow at the centre of my palm
as a speck where two lines meet
as you grow in the dawn ice glittering under a streetlamp
and in the stare of a startled cat
caught by a sweeper's broom behind rubbish bins.
You enter me from an open window
of a club where men are playing chess
or from a lone drop of rain
that brushes my left eye.
A driver adjusts his mirror.
A woman on an early morning bus
reapplies her lipstick.
Gently you take shape
like two letters on a kiosk's newspaper banner
marrying for the first time
with a steady indrawn breath
unheard in any human language
or you click behind me all at once
as the faint shudder of sound
that stumbles out of a dream fragment
to reappear as a car brakes.

My heart is light
as I walk with this chip of infinite mystery
rushing to the place where I must be
this morning.

## Conversation while waiting

Who has gone furthest away from me?

Is the sky to be trusted
and, when I die,
will my feet point left or right?

It is night now
and the trucks delivering forgiveness
and frozen fiestas
have still not arrived.

Can the hidden alphabet
be made plain?

A few steps beyond the deserted esplanade
light and the reassuring hum
of distant planets vanish.
Far from me
the waves withdraw, muttering
an unknown language of intimate collapse.

I am waiting to enter
the rollcall of their
magnificent thunder.

## ALLY BURSTON

# Argentine Tango

In a world where the waltz
is a distant dream,
the history of us
plays on
between the violin strings;
coursing through muscle
through kicks and flicks.
One, two, three, four.
Slow, quick, quick, slow.
Hush.
And caminada.

The fabric of my dress slivers
like smashed confetti
across the ballroom floor.
The angles of our legs
intertwined
like a black widow's web
entrancing, wicked, and you beg –
but this dance is for me
and you're my puppet.
One, two,
silhouette.
Three, four,
I see visceral red.

The audience has gone
but we still reign the floor
beware the black queen;
she will always kill her king
and darling, you've fallen
into her spider's web.

Our feet glaze the floor, sequins
coming loose.
My mind drifts
to when you would lift
those golden girls
in a bold sentada
as I sat in maddening want.
"You must deserve the tango,"
You had said.

The violin strings
reach their sharp crescendo,
bringing me back.
I curve my legs
to align with yours,
the contours of my jaw
accompany yours.
And that mask you wore,
with all grandeur and poise,
falls off with that Latin voice
rising to my ear to say:

## "Darling"

And I smile.
One, two,
I spin to kick you.
Three, four,
you land on the floor.

And I saw red
in your eyes.
Flashing, visceral
red.

## Charleston

She lifted a cheap cigarette to
her scowl-encrusted lips, took a long
drag, began to sweat. It was hot
outside, and I saw her hundred
year old eyes recede into the back
of her head. She would often do this,
Sylvia would. Begin to backtrack and
forget the years that had passed.
Just once, just this time, I sat
my young body down next to hers
on the nursing home terrace.
And closed my eyes.

Smoke traced the heavy air as
a trumpet played – a soundtrack
to the river of liquor that flowed.
It was night but it was morning.
A Manhattan speakeasy drenched in glitter
and stolen gold. The women sport chopped
bobs with a satin band; their drop-waist
flapper dresses doubling the room
as they Charleston danced.

Men in penguin suits, the first of their kind.
They perform a godless dance with a
dark-eyed Cleopatra in rhinestones and feathers.
But a feather gets stuck in one man's sweat;

The Great Gatsby of this old woman's head.
He grabs the string of pearls wrapped
around her glistening neck. Pulls her off
to the crowded sides, and she slaps
his callous hands – all she wants to do is dance.
So he glides her to the centre
while Zelda Fitzgerald played. His glass
eyes spot his rivals; those bachelor war vets.
Each one with an eye on his prize;
his painted lover's stocking legs.

It was the hip-hop of the '20s, but
the music could not compete
with the brawls of circus men.
Zelda stopped crooning and rebellious
girls stopped their animation.
The Russian roulette had started;
bullets raining down
in an All That Jazz variation.
Her Gatsby rung a shot,
sent them back – déjà vu.
His Cleopatra choked, tried
to reach for air
blown from the shriek whistles
of those uncool boys in blue.
The smoke was heavy now;
blood-stained dresses confused my mind –
sun shone through my eye lids,
turning me blind.

"He was always like that."
Sylvia shifted in her beige gown.
The foolish, rich old man had died
choking on his own vomit five years past.
Sylvia's permanent bruises
had famously vanished – her bright eyes
coming to life again. Sometimes, she
would dance, hop around,
swinging a leg or two out.
It would always infect her mind,
that drunken Charleston dance.

# The Castle

A man is knocking hard, unannounced, hoping
to make an appointment. He greets me as I return
from the library skirting mud, the damp grass.
Mary, the housekeeper is down with flu, our chef
is pumping weights at the gym. You are on a train
to London, a priceless alibi. And I, a village girl
in stockings, could be your messenger. I call to say
the surveyor has arrived to make an appointment.
Why can't he be a surveyor, today?— I have in mind
a poem about Kafka's *Castle* but my sympathy turns
from Amalia to the vacant, water-damaged lodge,
where the carpet has been stripped and is ready
to be trashed like spam. While the man talks about
rewiring, I'm in your chair, surrounded by piles
of signed, handwritten letters from hopeful fellows.
I fail to mention rain dripping like sap from the lintel
beyond the drawing room where the river Esk
decants, bending back on herself, a gift returned.
I should pack or throw away tickets, receipts, maps
and pamphlets I've collected, but that seems dull,
a reminder of petty anxieties. Last night an invoice
arrived from Vodafone in two different countries.
I should take a walk along the river but can't face
the ice wind, the day's camera obscura, dark pines
along the ridge, the river's braided veins, the cold mare.
*When are you coming back?* you asked, last week.
*I'm leaving tomorrow. Not waiting for the taxi. Not yet.*

Yesterday, as we were blown to the tower, its corseted
window and gouged wall, snow beat against our faces,
too bitter for grief. *If you fall out there in the cold*
*you could die.* There's no point resisting: we can't stay,
each one of us, though what we seek is rest, we are restless.
The trees swither, say stop, soon the light will be lost.
I could walk by the river, even now— it's not too late.

## How the Dusk Portions Time

Then one evening, after the gallery, hung with invisible
abstracts, you take me apart to flesh the miniatures:
a fleck of craquelure, speckles of mascara from my
shadow eyes, already panda-streaked.

I fail to notice how you slip the pieces in your coat pocket.
Distracted as I am by wolf hands, the hairs in your cleft
neck. You're not, but you might be, up yourself, I think,
skating across the vestibule floor.

How the light divides the dream, menacing, promising
shyness or indifference, I cannot tell, though it amounts
to the same verdict. Is that what you mean about pleading
guilty as the fig trees stir, balmy in winter?

Some evenings are this fragile. Rainbow lorikeets court
the soft crumbs, a magpie takes off with a crust, clouds
skim over the Finger Wharf, footsteps trip in the Domain
where the pine scent lingers as lips:

ours for a flower moment, the botanist's pinnate rose
is a name calling to its mute echo. Bats skip and loop
the legible sky in their quiet frenzy like involuntary
kites between metallic and neon spires.

So dusk emulsifies desire, or maybe it's the reverse
—we are tenants of this periphrastic end. Office cubicles
half-lit, ladder the sky, turning their discretionary gaze
          to what's sketched by the carbon ink.

## Celestial Meeting

Gather up your needles, my sisters,
gather up your thread. Tonight
we pierce the eyes of our needles
by the light of the half-moon.

The Weaver Girl is weeping
and the Cowherd leans on his staff.
The children flank their father
and try to blink away their sorrow.

The Goddess tore the night sky open
with one stroke of her pin. The stars
rushed to fill the void and formed
the Silver River. Once a year – and only once –

on the seventh day of the seventh month,
the magpies of the world forget their jewels
and wing their way above the clouds. They form
a shimmering constellation, a celestial bridge

for the meeting of the Weaver Girl and the Cowherd.
Bright-eyed as magpies, in the half-light
of the moon, by the glow from these embers,
we thread our needles, and sew our wishes on this silk.

*Notes:*
*The Qixi Festival, which takes place on the seventh day of the seventh lunar month, has been celebrated since the Han dynasty (206 BC – 220 AD).*
*The myth of the Weaver Girl and the Cowherd can be traced back 2600 years. It was recorded in the poetry classic* The Book of Songs, *comprising works from 11 to 7 BC.*
*The Weaver Girl represents the star Vega; the Cowherd, Altair; the Silver River, the Milky Way; the bridge of magpies, the Cygnus constellation over the star Deneb. In folk religion, the Weaver Girl is a minor deity worshipped by young women, in the hope that she bestows upon her followers dexterity in needlework, physical beauty and a good marriage.*

## Secrets

*for Louise Potter*

Two women are speaking
of the forbidden. We are
in a car, driving along a highway,
cows dotting the countryside;

we are in a café, looking
over our shoulders for ghosts.
We speak, our voices melding,
our volume rising. We laugh,

revelling in the fact that we can,
that we still exist: intact, mended.
When we speak to each other
we place our hands on our hearts,

reminding ourselves they still beat.
We drink tea at the factory
under the vines. We tell our secrets.
They fill up the whole of the sky.

# A Sensible Miracle

Punctiliously, each attended
to the other. Listening with care.
Concerned. Neither so much as murmuring
out of turn. Familiar voices from an alien past
had allocated roles to us by gracious intimation,
directing our conversation with the order
and the pattern and the precedence of dance.

That we had formed to voice at all
seemed then a miracle
conferring on our talk a quiet pride,
for we had triumphed over obstacles:
our ignorance of each other,
otherness, and a multitude of others'
expectations, hovering.
And while the absence of distrust does not,
in truth, amount to trust,
somewhere between the terror and the table,
the entree and the mains,
distrust was overcome.

Courtesy, as respect and disciplined compassion,
finds freedom there from incivility and insult.
And exposure. Had control, or even meaning,
been relaxed or compromised
a fragile understanding would have shattered.
Or so it seemed to me. The snakes,

the ladders of experience, the rituals
of gentleness and gender,
gave ample space for edited confessions
and temperate repartee
to draw their breath at leisure,
so to speak, without fear
of hyperventilation.

There are some, no doubt, will want to know
if anecdote or observation did not
reach out
in the sharing: "Did not your words",
they'll say, "just once, like harbour waters,
surge or swell beyond intention?
Your hands, by accident or cunning, brush
and prophesy a breach of ritual?"
"Did no involuntary vulgarity escape
to storm the castle you had built
so circumspectly in the air?"
"Was there no passion", they will ask,
"and did no intimacy dare
insinuate itself?"

No.

None of the clumsy choreography
of adolescent love. Two sensible
human beings, we parted
friends, well met and innocent
of awkward, empty pleasures.

## Ode to the Sparrow

Of all the most grand things: issimi; schemes;
Ees and pianos; iloquents; larcenies —
Grandleast the truckle and pipcrotch Esparrow
On the hip-hop engobble, or come-a-crop breeze.

Bird only ever wert, orni and malapert,
Graceful thou never wert, chirrup nor charmest,
Spirulent, rather, with windfalls to spare
For Aurora: oscuroclast; feathered alarmist.

Breakfirst to wake first, O sparrow, good on yer!
From inside your element you stir the unborn:
O bird, worth your word in the wings of the lingo
Where inside your aliment you warble out dawn.

## KERRYN COOMBS-VALEONTIS

### crackling my yellow!

*"colour is wounded light"*
— william blake

wattle time crackles my yellow
busting the breaking of
its own spell-
crazy for the spring

blissballs of fluffy
riot against coldness
public display of affection
resplendent in rapture

exultation
must be yellow as
the breast of that robin
claiming the last song of

dusk locking up the colours
bursting your yellow with
full-frontal flashing
its refusal of drab

yellow alive
blake's colour-of-joy wounding the light-
crackling, yelling your yellow;
that colour yellow!

# you big empty (nest)

you big empty
hanging on the horizon, blowing my house down
you big nothing
swallowing the curtains on the bared windowsill
you big turbulence
robbing my nest of fleece wrestled from barbed wire
and gossamer woven from soft feathers pulled
the wind scours and scatters
you big silence
yawning as you stretch your legs out by my fire
you big empty
burning down, filling the quiet settling in
the bottom of the chair

## The Black Dog

How innocent.

First thoughts like a child's simplicity of mind.

Momentarily there is freedom.

Mere seconds this time. Freedom nonetheless.

There is something in the corner.

Looming.

Controlling.

Somehow forgotten in the ignorance of slumber. Suffocating memories slip through the cracks of a fragile mind.

Conscious to a stomach now twisting with knots. Flittering and fluttering of delicate wings.

Tendrils of blackness penetrate. Clinging to every fibre of being.

Carefully step into your refined façade.

Smile when necessary. Laugh when appropriate.

How are you?

Are you okay?

So easy it is to believe your own white lies.

## 10 Verden Close

Down the hill traversed so often
a well-known tree, though sometimes more.
Lacklustre to those who couldn't know better.
Small. Simple. Secluded.

Oozing with possibility, endless realities.
This place is rich with significance.
Subtleties of every nook and cranny,
Familiar to me like the back of my hand

No knock as I enter, though this isn't my home.
Welcomed as one of their own.
*United again my accomplice and friend*
Ever ready to pick up where we left.

How can there be any care in the world?
When this world adapts to our will.
This place is for us and always will be.
For now, at least it would seem.

Ten years on still sharp in my mind
how important a dull place can be.
Nostalgia, not always a comforting thing,
10 Verden Close – the last time I was free.

LUCY DOUGAN

## The Shy Dog

*Our customary visible order is not the only one. It coexists with other orders...Hunters are continually aware of it... Dogs, with their running legs, sharp noses and developed memory for sounds, are the natural experts of these interstices.* (John Berger)

The shy dog will only come to me,
to a female voice.
The vet says it's all down to the kennels,
her handler.
My fingers explore the small ridges of her skull
and we are shifting into a landscape of grasses,
moving with the tribe.
Or, I am very young again
and up in the attic
reading Henry Treece;
travelling for days with the men,
never leaving my bed.
The Icini queen burns London, Colchester, Verlamion
and claims the hero with swinging plait and blue skin,
her palm warm on his thigh.
Later, I tried this move on a boyfriend
but he didn't, like the hound, take me for a natural leader.
At least this...
My son, who is currently berserker,
would have some place out beyond the dog,
a forward scout,
crazy enough to take the necessary risks.

And I think, too, of my father's death.
How removed we are from that fierce place
except for the Discovery Channel.
I wanted a bier, fire.
I wanted to decorate with gold teeth, spoils
he told me to claim at the end.
With the shy dog,
watchful for my next command,
maybe I could have just done that.

## Julia, Reading

Belly down on the graveyard lawn,
you balance the court shoe
you have just thrown off
neatly between two feet,
engrossed in a book
with your father's reading face on.
Small white flowers dot the lawn
and the gravestones, leaning
willy-nilly like bad old teeth,
stretch beyond you.
Here the parish let the place go wild,
left hides for foxes,
free passage for any number
of skittering things.
Good, we think, these dead are not lonely.
And I love it that you can
lie here on the grass so casually alive
and lost, no doubt, in some current franchise.
The small of your back is just bare
and the soles of your feet catch the light.

Now your feet have outgrown
these kitten heels,
sensible purchase from a stalwart aunt,
so I wore them all next winter
in another hemisphere,

walked the thin lining of black suede
off their backs.
They are good for gardening,
dashes to the shops;
and I find I cannot throw them out
because in them rest
your hair glints on that day,
a big untidy bunch of yellow flowers
left by a grave,
and St Witta's bones at Canonicorum,
if you bound up suddenly,
just steps away.

## Jupiter

The harbour's idle undulations slew
And swill their slicks of glaze to make
An unimaginable shape in time
The mind would ache
To contemplate. Above, small figures climb
The bridge, aspiring to a simpler view.

Down on the upper deck of the toy ferry
Now sliding underneath that span,
Deep in today's political polemic,
A businessman
May miss the news that renders academic
That puppet show, and makes unnecessary

Proposals he is anxious to embrace,
Initiatives already planned,
Between the tropics and the poles, between
The Ice Age and
The Holocaust, juju and mutant gene,
Planck's constant and the curvature of space.

Tethered in mid-Pacific still revolves
The dateline, dealing out the days
Like there was no tomorrow. Each of them
Plays and replays
Self-replicating hours— a theorem
Of endless present it propounds and solves.

And here, out from the shadow of the bridge,
The ferry surges into this
Ceramic swash, whose crazing would defy
Analysis.
The businessman reads on, but you and I,
Illiterates of trade and leverage,

And risk too intricate for even Lloyd's
To cover, simply watch the slurs
Of gloss and shifting craquelure. They say
It's Jupiter's
Vast mass that draws off, and may hurl our way,
A terminating hail of asteroids.

## Night Music

The night's blank alleys and blind passageways,
The darkness visible of ruptured sleep,
The hours with their stretched-out and wrung distortions,

Like faces in a funfair mirror—all
Pressed close about this shape of grief. These gaps
And oubliettes and vacuum-sealed displacements

In what I'd once call thought, and thrumming with
The scratched insides of silence and what isn't,
These hollow sockets of each gouged emotion

Grinding their iridescent insect noise,
Their bitter nothings in my skull— they all
Lay down with me.
                                        One night I took to bed

Debussy's works for piano, all five discs
Placed round the CD player's tray, all five,
No, more than six surrounding hours. I pressed

First Close, then Play, and then turned out the light,
And went to bed, all eyes in that annulment,
And waited for what might become to come—

The music's heavy water, so I hoped,
Finding its level, seeping in slow flood
To fill and flush those shrill obsessive chambers.

And so, disc one, those stately chords, *Pagodes*
Lapped over me. And wave on wave began
The night's long-playing, alternating phases

Of drowse and wakefulness, the periods
Of indeterminate extent when I
Was absent from myself—or finely snagged

On one still fizzing wire of consciousness
Which pulsed behind the notes its faraway
Demented siren song— then might float up

Midway through *Les collines d'Anacapri*,
Disc two, those runs like startled birds, or hear
Only that whir when disc flicked through to disc.

*Brouillards*, *Bruyères*, *Feux d'artifice*, brief lapses
To doze, and brief arousals, then a deep
Immersion in insensibility

Relinquished by the harping mind, at length
To surface in disc four, towards the end:
*Pour les accords*. Another whir: disc five,

And *Clair de lune* illumining the room
With a sonic shimmer of forgetfulness.
In one of the innominate small hours,

Succeeding *Elégie*, that final click.
Borne on the music, I went silent too,
My sleep a slowly fading pedal chord.

## The poem must

resist the intelligence almost successfully

— *Wallace Stevens*

I'm dawdling. Killing time. Or time
is killing me. That's an elegant city building.
Eight storeys high. Art Deco? Art Nouveau? Composed,
balanced. Deep set verandas, featured brickwork,
bay windows facing east. But who lives there? How
do they do? Or next door, forty storeys higher
in the skyscraper, the literal and the metaphoric
literally fused in glass and steel. Other lives
are closed to us. To me. What do they imagine
looking down from such a height? Am I just
a bald patch which reflects the sun? Cosmologists
promote and demote planets, endlessly dispute
definitions of a galaxy and complicate beyond intelligence
our earthbound understanding of the heavens.
No surprise then that the poem pretends
to be a bee, a bird, the cosmic wind
raging round the surface of the sun. Just last Saturday
a full moon rose all stark and staring,
all high-vis orange, out of a darkening sea
and we stood ranged along the headland
like a line of bonobo monkeys, mesmerised . . .

## The right time to write

is when you have nothing to say

— *A. R. Ammons*

Sixty young women bend to legal studies papers
on a day predicted to be fierce with heat.
Time splutters and almost stops, I almost fall asleep,
girls squint and frown and do their best
to ease a stiffening back or flex cramped fingers.
The fans are circling slowly and it's not
unpleasant, though the word 'oppressive' springs to mind.
Outside the wind gusts suddenly and thrashes
through the maple leaves. Sixty pairs of eyes,
and mine, turn to stare and, in a too brief
history of time, we even smile. Real time,
Stephen Hawking says, is a figment of imagination
and imaginary time is real. No time, I say,
too much time, looking for distraction, my mind
skittering, looking for something to latch on to . . .

## These presences come softly

*for Marshel*

These presences
Like evenings before the sunrise come softly
Jostling memories, spilling
A broken monologue

Long twirling, rolling lines
Like marbles splitting colours touch my mind
Fragility has no fragrance
Just colours of prayer, solitude and presence!

In the candlelight
The shadows are softer,
Making contours, spattering fragments
Making shapes that dance nilly-willy

Fingering the specked light
There grows in me something unrehearsed -
commotion ... emotion ... images ricochet posturing aliveness
Flooding a symphony of remembrances

And the roses pert and proud speak to me
Of the softness that touched your eyes (solemn though)
In the last glances we shared
Without words, without fear!

What is this language we found in sorrow?

This fearlessness at the edge of time!

A tribute to music perhaps... or poetry
Learning to pray in a foreign tongue
*Avvon d-bish-maiya*
Our heavenly father hallowed be thy name...
*O'shwooq lan kho-bein*
[leave us] leave us serene!

Let prayer dignify my grief.
*Avvon d-bish-maiya*
Ah ...– min!

These presences come softly.

## My last gift

*for Marshel*

When the dew from my eyes rests
It rests deep and unconscious…

I imagine

In the satin folds of my last gift –
I chose it carefully working through shades of colours and scents
Knowing it must speak of meanings and histories and bonds amorphous now –
And I lead us, our brood of eleven through the Vigil hour
Holding my last gift, longer than I should –
And when I lay it, I lay it softly … so softly beside you –

Not in the cradle!

A mural in my mind's eye!

And I think it was tutored long before this season,
Prepared deep beyond the veil for such a time as this!

And poetry now shapes my Vigil hour
And someone reads from the Gitanjali
'said the dew-drop to the sun' …
'What is there…'

And I think… what else?!
Only Gibran's farewell!

And here, NOW – the sun is rising
As I watch a solemn pantomime for you in Mt Roskill –
And I imagine a concerto on Ayers Rock to the beat of iambic verse
And a chorus waiting to be named –

It is enough you were my brother –

Hallelu-jah, Hallelujah … Hallelujah!

## Ash

*Cameron Allan (1955-2013), classically trained composer and musician, produced the initial recordings of many Australian bands, such as Mental as Anything and Icehouse, and composed soundtracks for several seminal Australian films. He migrated to the USA in 1986.*

Under the weather, the boat sways.
Your brother holds you for a moment,
then casts you out, all at once,
into the place where your parents
were cast, your parents who are long dead
now. You drift in the cloudlessness,
the gleam, and the sea sorts through you,
disperses you, though something
of a finer dust lifts on the swell.
Your brother has nothing to say.
He scatters into the tide the crushed things
he's felt for you, that aren't so easy,
and they dally there, like petals.
There's a sober quiet, a reckoning.
He recalls how, years before, you talked
of your mentor who came to see
he would never be Stockhausen, who unfastened
his life, drink by drink, until there was only
blood and regret. *Of course*, he says,
*I should have seen what was coming,*
meaning you, Cameron, drinking your life
away, you who were not Stockhausen.

But we all know this boat, the thump
of the waves on the wood, the hollow
of the hull, the hold of the sea and the sound
of the gulls, the sounds rearranging
as if by chance, becoming this song
always in our heads, this song of a possible
self. Atonal, perfect, lingering. This lovely, frail song.

## Season of Mist

*for Dylan and Kate*

Sitting in the half-dark,
in the pallid tones of *Casablanca*,
you asked me *Dad, when did*
*things go colour?* Not quite
listening, I talked about television,
my first small black and white box.
But that wasn't it. You stared
at the monochrome curve and said *No,*
*I mean the world. When did the world go*
*colour?* I think I laughed and you
went quiet, I think, and felt silly.
I didn't hear the colour in your voice.
Now, I'd tell you colours come
and go, they surge when there's love
and scatter like a shoal of fish,
startled, when the heart runs dry.
                                                  As you stand
in the heat of your wedding,
colours are swarming and swerving:
the bridesmaids flaring sun-yellow
beside cool aqua groomsmen;
the sea-blue suit you wear
and that white in her dress (don't
let pedants tell you white is no colour),

that white like a snowfall,
and the blush of your tumbling vows.
Afterwards, late rain, the slate
clouds shuffling about in the dusk,
feigning importance, like your father
perhaps, stirring the pot of the past,
clutching your mother's hand
and thinking of summer seas,
cerulean waves and star-white sands.
Spring pastures, their fizzy lime. The leaves
as they flush and fall. The days getting shorter, and dark.

## Letting Go

I dream of a white kite with bows on its tail.
Ardent, it rears. Tenacious —
an impulsive face-off with the wind,
until it dives for cover.

Aware of its weakness it distracts with a dance —
fluidity and elusive motion.
With instinct electrified my limbs bumble
playing catch-up until
grass cuttings cradle my back.

White knuckles and clenched mind.
The white kite tugs,

my fingers uncurl
one
at a time.

ANITA GERSBACH

## Where do unicorns come from?

Aurulent sunlight hovers delicately in the air
brought to life by gleaming specks.
Like a held breath, a fractured moment
floating loose from its source,
for that second the earth is afire with fairy dust
and the moon is made of cheese —
I think I'll grab my jar, slip a beam inside
and save it for a cloudy day.

## Old Tunes

Here are the old tunes
the way we always used to play them:

the slow chords
of philosophy,
the tireless rhythms
of creativity,
the cadences of caring.

Here they are –

the staccato of heart
and mind,
The tied notes
of silence,
The million fluted notes
of joy.

Do not be careless, and forget.

For one day
you may find the written score
that was ourselves

and long with all your heart
for the sound of its return.

## ALTHEA HALLIDAY

### Autumn in Thiele Court at Barker

Wind that moves
the shadows on stone
that cracks the leaves
and shakes the trees

You speak to me

softly
hesitantly
silently.

Sometimes
when it is summer
and not now
you shake your fist
in my face,
you shout at my window
and bang on my door.

The children cower.
The dog runs in for shelter.

But that is then
And this is now.

Now, it is autumn

with an azure sky
and leaves largely yellow.

Now there is sunlight
speckling on sails
and late azaleas
and white gardenias.

And poets.

And poetry.

# CLAUDIA HOUSTOUN

## She's a reader

I eat words all day
teeth crush consonants and fricatives into ice-shards,
they sluice over my brain and chill the back of my mouth
some exit there and spatter into breath
others trickle down my legs
and pool in my toes, seep through the floor
there are vowels too
some match-make and gestate and birth dipthongs
the plosives and affricates compete tirelessly,
claw up my lungs and lasso my tongue
hold it ransom with knotted retroflex ropes and stops.
Sounds are glass-in-oil,
they devolve to introspection, indoors, whiskey
but letters always find me, send
smooth vowels
ply with sonorants, sibilants, trills and liquids
seduce with innumerate constellations of
twenty-six elements
and I seek to net perfect words until
they slingshot breath into space

## Destruction

Upon dormant snowdrops
among oak roots
Mum drags a hose, watering

I sit, small hands search
pop hats from acorns
press leaves to dust,

find onions, with
robes of golden butter-pastry:
divested, fibrous white flesh

shoulders, navel, layers.
I strip them until emerges
the indivisible nucleus.

Vestments scattered
around my dirty knees
French Onion soup

*Onions*, I mutter
*My bulbs*, she sighs and waters

## JASMINE HUNTER

# Trafficked

Sweet and full of sparkle
but snatched up
during their twelfth year of life.
Twelve.
The average age of girls
who accept this oppression
as a career.

Gender inequality,
the deep roots of this
criminal enterprise.

I can write,
but I'll never understand.
It's their stories
I'll write to make a statement,
be their mouthpiece,
be of aid in this battle,
hopefully.
But that is all.

# Ochre House Emerald Fields

A tapestry of intertwined memories—
sunlit ridge and treetop fortress,
fields of grass waving in the breeze.
Acacias planted by hands
quivering in hope of
golden orbs to come.

Gardens incite mischief.
Bamboo begs to be crafted
by clumsy fingertips.
Arrows launch,
preceded by cheeky grins.
Brothers engage in battle
when adventure bursts inside
adorning walls with crimson clay.

Within the ochre walls
siblings play pretend
under recycled timber stairs.
Crouched amongst the clutter
they build a home
complete with the scent
of damp earth rising from
the manhole below.

SOPHIA HUSBAND

Dusk melts to evening and
adventurers retire, seeking solace
by the glow of the fire.
Here the years pass
as she dreams and
acacia blossoms

## Welsh Embroidery

*Trowch eich*
*wynebau attaf*
*fi holl gyrrau y*
*Ddaear fel ych achuber*

she stutters—
Welsh imperfect
but meaning clear

passed from mother
to eager child
over three hundred years

Granma bids me go
points with fingers curled
to her framed embroidery

I trace the script
feel the fabric, faded
and raw, and realise

long before I knew,
*I knew*,
etched on my heart—

'Look unto Me
the rest of your days
and you shall be saved.'

## Contradiction

On occasions I see you through old windows, now rotten,
A diaphanous ghost, drifting smoky and thin,
And my memories arise among tears long forgotten,
Like a love than has been,
Like old loves than have been.

I am reaching for you, hells and edens are shaking
I am grabbing them trembling, knowing well that I'll die;
And I feel you afar, for my body is aching,
I am longing to cry,
I am longing to cry.

I have pushed you away, but I wish you beside,
You're my lifelong desire, though for death I implore,
You enslave me with memories, you submit as my bride
Whom I love and abhor,
Whom I love and abhor.

## Diva

When the concert came to an end
I rushed to get an autograph.
But such miracle did not transcend
and despite being worshiped like a golden calf
the diva left in a hurry
leaving me with memories,
some vivid and some blurry,
but most of all with that
stunningly smooth canyon
between those mountains made out of molehills
I went home,
so stop looking at me, as you give me the chills,
rolling your eyes and shaking your head,
just because I went inside my shed,
to briefly fan my firefly.
I went inside proudly and walked out quite shy.

# Exotic

Perfect in Dublin's Botanical Gardens
the tulip beauties celebrate themselves.
Like teasing girls they stare and sway.
I turn my reluctant back on them
to walk for ages amongst plants of
every wonderful shape and shade.

But here is the true exotic of the day
growing wild in the hothouse of the café.
Among the doughy conversations,
shots of coffee grain laughter
and tea cups whispering steam,
a young boy alone at a table moaning,

rocking on the short stalk of his body,
swivelling his head from side to side,
his blind and shocking eyes
cobalt flowers without stamens.
Propped cross legged on a chair,
he drools and croons, a hybrid.

We around him fresh from our garden walks
politely dig at dainty morning treats
with little silver forks
and swallow pity and relief
in equal parts, unsettled,
eyes anywhere but there.

Mother and father return with cafe trays.
Root stocked to their voices
his rocking moaning works a pitch that pierces
every corner of a room now stilled.
Dadda!
He shouts his solitary word, exalts it.

Tenderly the father feeds his son, scooping food
into a mouth no girl will want to kiss.
The mother smiles and leans across
to wipe a crumb from her husband's cheek.
They flare like the tulips,
suddenly lovelier.

## Codes To Leave

The late flush dahlias flare
like little disappointments.
A desultory carer smokes outside.
There are codes to enter here.

The place smells of yesterdays.
The looks are single outward journeys
shuffling each day's future tense
into something more speculative.

This is a harsh final surrendering.
In Room 23 are your codes to leave.
You have come down to this world.
You are small now,

in this space.
Did you lift me, once,
over salty breakers at Bar Beach
where horizons rolled?

In the corridor even the light echoes.
My too loud voice is gauche.
You are moving into a silence.
All day you will stare at the wall clock.

At Steinbeck's ending
I break from my reading
and weep silently
for you my father.

You say
*this is the natural order of things*
and get on with the hard work
of your dying.

I am thinking of continuance
when I take your jacket to be cleaned.
They will dress you in it
at the funeral parlour.

Some weeks later
still in my handbag
five grapes in cling wrap
unravel me.

## Night gardening, mauve and mutable

One a.m., an alcove opens to show a back lit slipper orchid,
then closes. The orchid had slipped off eleven years before.

The sweet pea seeds that did not make their planting
date with Saint Pat's, bloom midwinter in the sofa divots

while a startling halo of cherry blossom grows
on my head the night I came back from Bundanon.

I expect the ferns will not block the lower steps,
but that is their day job, they're only neat by night.

At two a.m. I set to with a spade and plant an acreage
of asphodel in a corner of the garden that day will not reveal.

Night root stocks are pure graft, the peach tree fields cherry pits
inside a plum dark flesh, the scent is apricot, like it too forgets.

The jacaranda blossoms give proof of coloured dreams, like a note
written in early sleep, here, take this as evidence.

The day time trees I planted, the lemon gum in Darlinghurst,
a winter crop of angophoras at Crafers, do I appear in their dreams,

trailing clods of dirt, leaving the scent of sweat from a damp
and dirty shirt, and broken vanes of windmill grass?

## Afloat

Floating curious in a dinghy, wondering
about the sea below, I take a corrective
drop of brine, place its lens in my eye.

Now I see perfectly through the bright aqua-
marine beneath me, the azure above
and from a distance off, the boat I'm in,

and how it displaces more than its weight
in saline, making its own meniscus,
as that drop now refloats mine.

## Someplace Really Good

A
Fallen
Leaf
Tugged from the tree
By October wind, after the bloom of flowers.
Thrown to the ridged ground with force, the stem snapped.
Stumbling,
the leaf battered by pavement
across the intersection between Corner and Parish.
The Avenue collected lost pieces, what's left?
A coffee brown body
For an acquired palate
What's left gripped together, holding on tighter to survive.
The wind rested. The city rested
And when the fallen leaf reached the end, it turned around and realized it ended up
Someplace
Really
Good.

# Red Door Blue Door

Parallel lives that never have touched
Two doors stand side by side
On Upton Street among the Maples
That grip tighter to survive.

One door opens as the other shuts
Two doors growing old
Whether weather wethers the paint
Or it's the lack of colliding souls

Behind the Red door a life is lived
A woman for an acquired taste
Follows the shadow of the second hand
Follows to Corner with haste

Behind the Blue door a life is lived
Governed by the clock
He steps in time with every stroke
To Parish he counts each block

Red door, blue door, patient gates
Wind still bits his tongue
He hears whispers of turning locks
And says, "Patience, due time will come.

When the big hand hits 'S' and the little hand hits 'oon.'
Red door and Blue door will meet
You'll have to wait until then, my loves.
Due time can be so mean."

If time is distance between two doors
With the two clocks out of stroke.
Then Blue door and Red door will never meet
Until the final ~~joke~~ line.

## Saint Kevin and The Blackbird

*I hope you love birds too. It is economical.*
*It saves on the need to go to heaven.*
—Emily Dickinson

Backlit, the winter blackbirds are dark clothes-pins
on bare branches, hanging small rags
of the low Irish sun out to dry.

In 618, Saint Kevin of Glendalough
found a blackbird
had landed on his palm
when his arms were outstretched in prayer.

He remained still
as the bird built its nest
brooded over
and finally hatched its eggs.

He survived, or so the legend goes
on the offered food and water from its beak.

The same Saint Kevin hated human kind
so demonstrably
he once threw a woman who desired
to marry him, over a cliff to her death.

So what is the lesson?

Is it just that one man's likeness of flesh
is another man's poison?

Or is distance itself the thing?
And God or bird
we may only worship something
so far apart from us
there's no chance
we'll ever understand it.

At some secret signal, the blackbirds in the tree
take flight in a heart flutter of wings.

Each denuded branch reacts by swaying
like the high wire at a circus
after the walker has stepped off
and onto the safety of the platform.

Five minutes later, the smaller twigs still swoon.

## Photography at Dingo Creek, 1967

Here's the telescopic shot. Her father drives
the Morris Hillman as if it is a tank.

She's in the back. Door handles rattle across
each *rackety-crack* of the wooden bridge.

Memory pulls over to the side of the road
climbs out and into a craze of farmer's friends.

The girl, at six, holds open the jaws
of barbed wire, gingerly, top and bottom

steps through leaving her small sacrifice
of dress or knicker material

then scrambles bum first or careless knee-bleed
face-down backwards descending

the red-bellied-black-snake bank
to the water.

She takes off her dress
the yellow spotted one, and those first

few second's immersion are so mountain-chill
small peaks erupt in the snow of her skin.

Caustic-lung, leg-burn and throb.
She dives, resurfaces. The blue-blind

pain disappears and she looks up
to see if he is watching.

It's been decades.

Her father's passed on
and the creeks are dry
            all the way to Mount George.

She recalls he never joined her.
Never allowed his arms to turn

over and over in the nothing-spilled
nothing retained
            perfect zen of swimming.

Instead his fingers were bent
to small safe-cracking circles

of lens and dial as he set up his tripod
on dry land then waited
for the perfect light to frame her in.

Intent on preserving
her childhood like the fossil

of some sea-going creature
found intact a million years on
in the desert.

Or if she was never found
it wouldn't be for the want
              of his trying.

On the back of each photograph
like a map co-ordinate

the recorded minute, hour, day
kind of filter, degree of exposure.

All the care it had taken
to trap her in the infinitesimal

shutter-speed wink
between the moment

and the moment's loss.

## Autumn sunset in Les Pyrenees

*September 13, 2014*

The autumn sun sets over her Pyrenean valleys;
this setting phased –
primal valley by primal valley;
stretching mountain peak by stretching mountain peak,
one at a time,
as she heads west.

But day lingers here around the clouds,
turning whiteness grey before pink;
deepening,
darkening the blue of the sky
as red tongues of sun flicker above the cliffs.
A final lick of warmth,
holding off the dusk
in this ancient place of grey stone.

The shrouding mist rolls down from the highlands
dewing, and hazing everything,
even the night,
until the morning.

The dog bark echoes from the broken crags;
he barks at himself,
over and over,

backwards and forwards,
around and around.

Beyond the stream
a grey wolf howls in the wind;
a brown bear trembles a branch.

By day, the colours of this place are at once true,
yet impossible;
unfathomable shades of tree greens,
turning golden at their tips overnight;
reddening to orange in a day.

The cobalt ever-ness of sky,
enfolding here, on earth.

Watching

steely cliff face and rocky ravine
guarding meadows of sentinel corn stalk;
of bowed and finished seed-shedding sunflower.

Cyclic life.

Wail of one lone bird at daily dusk –
mournful crone –
lost, still home.

## Suspended in Paris

*August 10, 2014*

Molten red sun setting ahead.
Translucent white full-moon rising behind.
The Seine;
and me.

A pivotal moment;
a hinge.

I am subsumed by nature:
suspended and teetering.
Embraced by beauty

in front;
lava-like shimmerings,
searing and sizzling,
slipping,
stealing the day.

Descending.

Behind;
chilly cold whisperings,
craving,
coveting the sky,
climbing the night.

Ascension.

The wonder;
so much enigmatic beauty
hanging in a glance.
Twice.

All around,
unfathomable power;
immeasurable potential.

Balletic synchronicity abounds,
amid day and night;
light and shade;
kind and cruel;
love and hate;
right and wrong;
nowhere and somewhere.

Away and home.

## to tend

to tend the gods as given, as found
new habits of homage are required

in word untamed, in sight unframed
paths to follow are so chosen,
by you, for you, willing, blind

go to the makers
not to the mockers
take the trouble to tell them apart

dust of the world you're sleeping off
lonely under feats of self
but work outlasts if you stay with the tune
survives you and the all-that-wearied

mockers, thieves and smug ignorers
in the end they scale away

so

get the toxins out of your system
protect yourself
protect your spark

light in the eyes may be derided
spring in the step, its menace is met

but you, brave maker
face the dark without, within

for you the tale untold doffs cap
the wheels take on their fated spin

if you'll remember one injunction

go to the makers
never the mockers

tend to the habits of homage

you've found

## advice for poets

worship the earth
the all we have
sun for warmth
and stars from which time
worship with hands
and love hands too
with the heart give
with each breath be given
do this with each word

JEAN KENT

## A Night Without Curtains

'I'll have to let the moonlight in tonight,'
my neighbour says, leaning out her undressed
kitchen window toward a twilight veil
of mosquitoes. Behind my about-to-bloom screen
of giant blue salvias, her curly head rises,
cratered with age but beaming
over the sage green leaves.

Before she lets the sun in, she shakes off
the shadows of leaves it has gathered
falling through wattles and gums.
She Japanese-gardens the footpath,
raking up every pawprint.

She leaves, normally, no leaf unturned.
But this is the first fine evening
for a fortnight, so now after neatening
her house, she hangs green mists
on her rotary clothes hoist. Outside her gate,
just for tonight, gravel sleeps
under wattle chenille. The juice of sunset spills,
staining us as we talk. Over the lake,
surprised by the sky's uncurtaining,
one star comes out to drink.

Laughing, my neighbour leans out …
then floats back. Though darkness sweeps
around the mulched ankles of my blue buds bending
and around my feet as I turn away …
I see tonight already
she has let the moonlight in.

## Translating a 'Prolog'

*for Rolf Hermann*

In the spring sunshine, under wisteria through the ironbark –
a sky of emphatic blue above, all around me
a bath of light –

While the tortoiseshell cat is sleeping, wound into a spiral
(on its wrought iron seat) of caramel, charcoal
and lime-white –

I'm trying to translate a German poem. Earlier the cat
sat on the dictionary. All English translations
of 'vertrauen' – 'to trust'? 'have confidence in'? –

disappeared under sunwarmed fur. Now she's confident
she's my mistress again, the purring bundle
settles in her own space –

leaves me to the foreign words in my hands.
Distracted, I hear a crackling under loquat leaves – breaking sounds
below all that my trees have shrugged off
in the last half year –

I wasn't here to rake them clear, and now the leaves
hide, then slowly release, a lizard that looks
like a sundappled creek –

a patient flow across the path, its flick of tongue
a lick of blue, in and out
of the light.

The reptile slides under another blanket of leaves
on a garden bed. The cat still sleeps.
From a forest of German

a snail in a cape of rain begins to wake.
On a book's bright field, oak leaves and acorns
scatter …

The blue tongue lizard when it blinks in the open again
is under the cat's dreaming chair.
Sunlight aspics them

one above the other, both oblivious, peculiar
as translations, shy gestures
towards another place.

# Facebook

A world of emotionless emojis
like carcases dressed as clowns
parading on a runway.

'Likes' equate to life fulfilment.

Pseudo friends—
the more the better.
We count the number
as a miser counts his gold.

A swamp of notifications,
messages disappearing through quicksand.
Strutting like a peacock—
gaining only stalkers.

The latest photo, status or comment,
sent out like a flare—
a plea from a sinking ship.

## My Map

The map on my brick wall,
stretched flat, held with Blu-Tack—
calls to my imagination,
igniting vivid 3D images

Beyond the blue, watery expanse
and colourful country divisions,
I glimpse red Zimbabwean sunrises
and catch whiffs of exotic spices,
floating through the smog of India

Splendid Mayan temples,
and the proud, jagged Himalayas,
rise out of my paper-thin map
as mighty warriors of time

Cheeky monkeys, stealing bananas,
and dancing women in saris,
flowing in Bengali breeze
invade my dreams

I become restless as
ocean currents pull me
through the salty waters,
to gaze upon Greece's calming
blue and white structures

## ANGELINA KERR

Flat paper, stretched
between two poles,
a canvas for imagination

The map draws me—
and I become
a vapour in the wind.

## Beached Dreams

*After Kenneth Slessor's "Beach Burial"*

Silently and gladly to the reefs of Christmas Island
the convoys of asylum seekers come;
at night they cling to the boards of wooden boats that roll
and list in heaving seas.

Between the fob and mincing of the sound bite,
no-one, it seems, has time for this—
to pluck them from a watery grave, wrap them in blankets
and raise a glass to honour

their remarkable courage, their very ordinary dreams
and their right to be proudly Australian. Instead,
we drive shards of broken tidewood into their beating hearts,
sealed by the signature

of our feckless leaders, written with such pragmatic
cowardice, with such unfeeling stubbornness
that the words choke as they begin—*Boat People*—
the ink bleeds and fades

in a sea strewn with the wreckage of decency,
the withdrawal of compassion, the failure
of a nation to face its fear, to understand that, like all of us,
they come in the hope of a better life.

*Nauru/Papua New Guinea*

## Waiting Beside You

All I can do is sit by your bed and watch you die.
I don't yet know that what I am feeding you
will become your last meal on this earth.

Spoon after spoon of thickened water because
it's easier to swallow and a few spoon*ful*s
of pumpkin soup, though spoonful is a misnomer.

Your appetite has shrunk along with your body.
Parched lips, eyes firmly shut, your white hair combed
back against the pillow. I watch your mouth slowly opening

as I balance the spoon and tip the clear, wobbling
liquid onto your tongue. Occasionally I miss and mop
your cheek with a tissue. You say, "Please"

and "Thank you" as if you have decided to teach
by example, impart the perfect manners that rarely
graced a table crowded with five boys who learnt

to eat quickly or go hungry. When I think of the word *mother*
I see you with an apron on, peeling potatoes, the black pot
simmering on the stove. I think how we took for granted

the steaming plates you placed in front of us, night after night,
how the kitchen was a no-man's-land you patrolled,
how peace was the sound of boys with heads down,

eating heartily. Everything has changed. Now we
can cook: goat curry, fish wrapped in banana leaves,
upside-down plum cake. Recipes are for sharing.

I lift the spoon to your lips and you say, "Thanks,
I've had enough." I listen to the rattle in your chest,
how each breath you take seems to fill up the room.

When I think of love I will always see a tablecloth—
knives, forks and spoons in their places, serviettes.
I will always hear your welcome cry, "Dinner is ready."

SHARNA KOSMEIER

## Priorities

It's 2am and I log on.
It's time I think to calculate.

I figure the figure is wrong
it says:
fifty five sad dollars,
and ten pathetic cents

should I have bought that book, those sunnies, that —

nail polish?

Half an hour later it's 2:05
still only 10 pathetic cents
Ah!

...Return the most expensive item to gain maximum returns and budget accordingly for the week, for the day,
anyway,

The Reject Shop had a sale on nail stuff and the
half-priced-tortoise-shell-cat-eyed-Ray-Bans meowed my name.
What a bargain!
But
Ninety-five dollars? For a textbook?

## SHARNA KOSMEIER

Well I never really was interested in
"Management and Cost Accounting" by Andreas Taschner and Michael Charifzadeh anyway

My glasses look fab…
how vital is this book?

I think the library has a copy

SHARNA KOSMEIER

## #veneer

I see her all the time
lustrous hair, it shines and bobs
as she strides and
her teeth shine too

we point at her
she is on point!
Brows
            Brunch
                        Booty

she carries fancy tea in a slim bottle with geometric,
flawless colours
the bottle reflects her like a mirror
in the mirror, she's liked

it's an art, something to study,
to look through the feedback of double taps and makeup hacks
it's visual news and her headline cries —
Attention!

yes, she is always smiling
on the screen, but
sulking in the car.

smooth skin is see-through when it masks a
fractured
heart

## The Twisthand

His was a kindly face
Rounded jaw
Eyes which twinkled like glow-worms
As he surveyed his machine
By the soft, even glow of candlelight
Scanning the soft cotton thread
Which formed the warp of this impossible web

His ears, too, attuned to the rhythmic thrump
Of his powerful charge
Could sense things out of kilter
As easily as an airport sniffer dog
Gentle fingers, long stained by graphite grease
Spent days guiding warp threads through near endless holes
In guide bars and Jacquard rig

Gargantuan machine now readied for work
With combs to guide
Exquisite brass bobbins in wafer-thin carriages
Each holding the finest Egyptian cotton the length of a football field
Back and forth, forth and back through forests of vertical threads
Twisting and knotting, dodging and missing
Making near mystical Nottingham Lace

This dark forbidding beast could weave
The stuff of dreams

RICHARD LANDER

Love of potentates, monarchs, queens
Yet still fresh princesses seek its soft caress
Beauty and the Beast in earthly form
Like Beauty's love the twisthand's sweat and tears had broken the spell
Revealing true beauty from deep within

## Renscombe Farm

It is the wind you notice first
That biting wind which finds every weakness
In your defences like a schoolyard bully
Slowly the salty smell of seaweed and rotting bait
Drifts from Chapman's Pool
Assaulting other senses

Eyes, nose, ears, deep frozen
Take in the ancient harvester
Trundling across Westhill Wood paddocks
Far below, steel-grey cliffs of Purbeck stone
And Kimmeridge shingle
Disgorge ancient ammonites at every storm
Same stone, torn from local quarries
Forms dry-stone walls, huts and homes
As chilling as the Renscombe wind

## The Beach

Whitewater surges towards you,
a hedgerow of small, liquid tongues.
You dive through to hissing
that sighs to a crochet of salt.
Diving, again and again,
you will come
to an endless slight rocking.
Here, light and water are one:
brief-slope and half-bowl striations;
light-tumblings, ruptures and pearls;
non-human hectares of dream-jostling,
skin-gentling slaps.
When you turn round
all you see's the huge light
flooding spray-drifts and stately, broad levels.
Unheard, waves crawl
across farther and farther gold sea-plains,
small, upper bodies
where great rays fan out
through the caves and suspensions of spray.

Later, you climb the warm stairs;
walk in and out through the shadows
that lean across bright, spongy grass, and pink paths.
Summer has soaked into crevices.
It sets at the back of your eyeballs,
bathes nerves in your scalp...

On, tired and slow,
past dark, wide-open entrance halls,
surfies, old couples with kids.

Side-streets that peel into jigsaw:
sky glimpses, leaf shadows, brick.

Bone-happy. Slow. Without utterance.

This is a gift from the sun and the planet.
This is not just something humans or words have made up.

## The Silence of the Frogs

So many silences.

Wharves. Or the silence of caves.

The silence of big skies. Of forests.

Of sunlight on carpet.

The silence of frogs.

You hear it round Sydney:
wherever the soil has been smashed,
or the billabongs drained;
wherever insecticide's crept, subtle tide,
into slicks where the pathogens bloom –
each distinct silence the shade of an absence –
a graph of what's no longer there.
You can walk through a loose, sandstone talus –
wind in the she-oaks, the black cockatoos
crunching cones; the peace-field of crickets
a torus with you at its heart: you will hear,
if you stop and breathe slowly, the diffident hush
where the bright, red-crowned toadlet once croaked.
Walk out in paperbark swamps at Kurnell –
through a patter of drips, after rain –

while shrike-thrushes start, and then mynahs,
and planes boost their thrust – you will hear,
in that open-air cave, the perfect
and brief non-existence of shy Wallum froglets.
Put on some boots for the leaf-litter – adders
and browns: the absence of burrowing frogs,
in the sun's empty air; the soundless vibrato
of bright green-thighed frogs; the fitful
but vanished staccato of stuttering frogs.

So many silences.

These are all new.

But they won't remain this clear for long.

They won't be so easy to hear
once this cohort of listeners is all silent too.

LYNNETTE LOUNSBURY

## gallery

art makes me want
to tear off my clothes
    all of them
    ripping them away
    shredding them
I don't. Because the women
with grey pixie cuts and black
edged frames and
pink explosions
    of lipstick
- they don't.
and they seem to be here a lot
they know. they know art.

in fact, now I can't remember why
I wear clothes
I want to touch the paintings
    With my tongue
I want to taste the colour.
when the fat man
    on the high chair
    is texting his mother
    I stroke the paintings.
bad art is the best
it smells like hope.

I settle. For peeling off my
hubris
and stacking it quietly in
          in the corner
nudity can be
metaphorical in a pinch
its adaptable like that.
if they notice - if they catch me.
I'll say it's art.

## Pragma

You say just do it, as though I can
Down tools
And write soft poetry
And sing wild songs of cushioned protest
As though I can
Knock off early
And save worlds and occupy important spaces
As though I am not tied, bound and ball gagged
To a reason.
As though revolution is not a rich, protected privilege
As though I am free -
When anyone who loves is never free.
Always a reason to compromise
Capitulate
Do as told
The sun here is bold, the trees have gentle claws and
Scrape free your memories
You forget the hostages.
The waiting mouths and open hands.
But I cannot.
I can see my reason in the night sky.
And people with a reason will never be the revolutionaries.
We don't want a brand new world
With no reason in it.

## Teralba

1. 1972

Life's sunlit.

A boy of four
doesn't reach far
not up the railing
above the trains here

waiting five minutes
or a week

lifted in his grandfather's
wiry arms, the warm crisp shirt
a heart there, lungs,
a stomach

the long shift done
steelworks far from the silverfoil lake

after, the train spills
flecked sun between the trees
curling south west
toward Toronto

twelve years left

waterbirds on the lake
in last light

2. 2014

The train slid through the trees
like the lake's waterbirds and shorebirds,
at dusk or at dawn, into the margin
between the water and the still-thin light
of the sky, nearly not there at all, the same light
over them, the birds seeming, for a moment,
to vanish, just before they do vanish.

The light, saturated with itself, streams
over everything.

My child sleeps on the back seat.

## South Maitland

Each scrap of hill
's an untidy fold
over the valley's long scarred seam

stitching Carboniferous swamps
to bush doof hearth fires.
The Hunter and some

of its bottle-deep creeks freeze in light
The mine offices go quiet
as old open cuts fill with boutique dams

surrounded by ti trees,
snake grass, burnt out car shells –
fenced-in against what? Roos?

Deals in the half-dark? The moon's
on one arc light in the repopulated water.
Online, the corporate history:

a map of bosses, mine heads and rail routes –
these are caves and cave-ins where
kids turn their ankles, and plumb how deep.

*

the towns scattered here
spent men at the mines

smoke falls from chimneys
vines linger at lane verges

men lose fingers
or worse under the ground

kids hurl around the old pits
mostly watching for where

the ground still is        at Pelaw Main
the red gravel and dirt    it slips

excavating the brick clay
left behind      Neath Beach

its reeds in shade
from the rail embankment

the creek's rust-red with tailings
leached from expired leases

its last corroded fish
turned ferric      not feral

Neath Road to Kearsley
digs through fog      past

the chitter dump     its flares and coughs
worry at parents

(*but what can you do?*)
rain smoulders through its slow

fire and makes dark pools
where it gathers          at dawn

when they dry     not
the colour of mud

hours of trains every night
from the sclerophyll

still shunt     whistle     tug
groan
that sounds about right

## Four

Mulberry stained fingers
Skipping through the door
Singing, hopping, slipping
Face down on the floor—

Blood and tears and screaming
An ice cream on my head
Three stitches through my face
I yell with every thread

A hat to school each day
To cover up my wound
Thought I'd be ridiculed
But the playground resumed

In healing I have found
The ground comes up so fast
A scar that tells the tale
Of slipping in my past.

# Thirteen

She chews, spits and crunches
Eyes like carnivore's teeth
Stories to bite, pages to swallow
Precious lives to keep

No care for daily tasks
No wonder where she is
Tearing down the shelves
Letters spit, splutter, whiz

Dragons, wolves and spears
Flowers and true lovers
Nothing's safe – ruthless claws
Scratching up the covers

Hardback skin, lettered spine
Paper for a mind
Inky skin and fingers
The library's where you'll find

A monster of the literature
Shelves never running short
No thing replaces stories,
The lessons that they've taught.

## Cards face up

Three are seated around each other:
an empty chair at the head of the table.
Fingers twitch – tongues dab lips.
Cards face up;
a game's in session.

Three cards – one for each sitting at the table.
One blinks like an owl, shoulders held high;
a black card rests in her palm—
a woman grasping a rudder in a sea of endless whispers.
Two drags fingers along the inside of his wrist;
a red card clutched in his fist—
a rotting apple rests on red silk, soft and warm as flesh.
Three blinded by a smouldering cloth, still grinning;
they hold a white card between two fingers—
a burning sword plunged through bleeding scales.

Filament burns and crackles in a glass cage.
A hurricane's eye haunts the table.
One blinks,
Two sighs;
Three smiles.

A whoosh of air—
The fourth player arrives and takes a deep
Breath
As the three bow.

## Sunshine

Day dawns and we taste the sun—
Dry mouths full of dead leaves or cold and crisp frozen ice petals;
That's what light *tastes* like.

The sun drifts forth and we listen—
Iced water dripping from loose fingers and the red sizzle of ants under glass;
That's what light *sounds* like.

The sun embraces a breeze far overhead—
Hot sand, stinging salt or dead grass mowed and rotting;
That's what light *smells* like.

Brushing skin as the sun sinks—
Gentle as a whispered kiss or tearing into flesh like cat's claws;
That's what light *feels* like.

Final rays find gazing eyes—
A baby's chuckles pink glow of sunrise, and halos of sunbeams at noon,
Whirling, burning shadows of red and the dark glow of hellfire at sunset;
That's what light *looks* like.

## Grandfather

In the warm smile of the fireplace
My grandfather sits
His faded denim eyes watching
The slow-dance of the shadows

Built like a mountain
A bushman's frame
With skin like the leather of an ancient saddle
Smoke and silver run through his hair

The fire chuckles softly
Horseman's hands loosen
My grandfather's eyes flutter
Like a magpie's wing

In the fading smile of the fireplace
My grandfather sleeps
Perhaps dreaming of a yellow truck
Or a red and white dress

## Day's End

The day grows tired.
Beneath skeletal frames of eucalypts,
Long black shadows stretch like snakes.

The light is fading.
Dipping lower toward the horizon,
The sun is a sinking ship of gold.

The clouds change colour.
Watercolour sky of yellows and blues,
To streamers of violet, tipped with flame.

The end is coming.
Daylight gives one final sigh,
Lets itself drown in the tresses of night.

DAVID MUSGRAVE

## The Field

I wake up in a field
curling like a fabulosity
you can see but not describe
That's what Poindexters are for
but in Poindexterese
among their abstractly gated
I can quote String Theory
neither do you but that's not
the view from 40,000 feet
to distinguish itself from dufus
or refusers like myself
I'm against it! Even me
of course   ripping at grass
at elegant angles hypotenusal
but that hasn't stopped me before
I take note all the time
apparently my poems are lists
(that's a different '—' btw)
including the fence which doesn't
which is delft blue
is in traffic or sentences
they don't obey or follow
embodies restlessness roadkill
something which is in them

of emerald dew and equations
of lips or string
in numbers or a new code
they can't describe in words
which they enjoy and share
communities           Hey —
but I don't understand it
a train wreck when you have
or whatever measure ego uses
users abusers Woolloomoolosers
Je refuse! Whatever it is
othelioma     There is a horse
tensile limps deployed
if that is a word
I'll take note now
menus shopping lists TO DO lists
but good lists according to —
and everything in this field
belong to me or the sky
or the ants which are as one
which meander under rules
but embody just as tar
emphysema   these ants know
but out of bounds

from ant school which is where    they're going    just like us
but in this field the rocks    are freckles on a personification
which I am uncomfortable with    but as random or necessary
as a metaphor or a signature    mine has never been satisfactory
I would have preferred to use    a pseudonym  your name perhaps
if you don't mind that is    but I mean my handwriting
like feathers or fish scales    or the frayed edges of blades
of grass listing lazily    as I watch and wonder
why I was asleep here    not to mention where I am.

## Climbing up

It began as a care-free thought
that she restlessly mused aloud;
her warm call beckoned me forward,
so we climbed the water tower.

Crimson signs cautioned approach
through ragged links and wretched barbs –
those haggard guards left unemployed,
shrugging shoulders to check our pass.

Then rung upon rung, bare toes curled
cold against the iron ladder, patiently
bearing guests to the summit
of its faded cream master.

A weary acacia looming lonely
above golden veld and morning bustle –
its bark-like lace tattered, frayed
by February scorch and August chill,

But its ken had stretched years
past the season's ebb and flow:
a weathered watchman keeping vigil
over that land I yearned to know.

# Time

What if waking, all the clocks had wandered away,
packing moth-eaten bags for a long-due escape?
Perhaps to those turquoise specks in the Pacific,
where deadlines and exertions are quickly banished,
flitting south on the back of some privy old seabird.

Surely a strike would follow those indolent sands,
as hands long and short wind up their old gripes -
red-cheeked protests to Earth's tired solar marathon,
compelled by the One whom tweed jackets crave debate.

Then the world might pause...and from habit hurry on,
pushing ever forward with its infinite race:
but if its laces were to poke through my window,
they would find only blankets, and *this* competitor at rest.

JAN OWEN

## A Little Wine

I remember you, Dario
courteous long-faced croupier
who found me lost in the mist
on Verona's vast piazza
with twilight rising from the cobbles
and how you escorted me back
through the blurred grid of alleys
towards my door, unsmiling
—yes, perfectly poker-faced—
but stopping on the way
'*per un bicchiere di vino*?'
at the counter of a small cantina
walled with bottles, a cellar come up for air.
And how a hand glanced off the lampshade
so it swayed just over the heads
of a dozen strangers like a benediction.
So the red wine, held up, sparkled on and off
and the warm Italian vowels
circled below the moving halo of light
around the invisible centre
of which we were
that moment, the tangible signs.

JAN OWEN

## Anticipation

The nosy dib, grub, moil
of a prickly neighbour
has razed another anthill
routing the troops – a spill
of broken rosaries that soon
rethread and reconnoitre to rebuild
with instinct, the overseer
directing the jet-black trickle's
spurt-stop-start.
It's an old film's jerky flow
this swapline of kiss:
one pheromone-tracking
flickering unit of formic work
that scoops and carries and stacks.
Team spirit is their religion
Many anticipating
One
the Tao of all such tiny mindful toil.

## Mother

*for my mum ~ I love you so*

I'm tiptoeing, teetering—quietly I witness
"*nanna, look...nanna, see*"
I don't want to move, do not disturb
magic is happening
not rabbits from black felt hats
not a rainbow of tightly tied ribbons
no, it's a pure magic
transcending the now

I'm transported
I am lifted, I soar to her height
her fragrance softly kissing me
her unruly hair caresses my cheek
her arms wrap me, I wrap her

My lips part, as if in gasp
I inhale not to be heard
not to be seen
no, so softly—to remind myself, I am here
not there

She looks up
she heard me, my near silent breath forever on her radar
"*mum, look...mum see*" It's unsaid

she smiles—an instant knowing, I am seen
a warmth radiates from her soul—I am aglow
I bask in it

They giggle
an eruption snatches my moment
I stand now in the shadows
not cold and detached
not hidden
no, shaded and protected

They giggle
she shines
her smile warms them, they bask
her eyes tell them, they know
her arms embrace them, they're safe

I'm there,
A sudden intake of breath
I remember
I close my eyes, not to not see
no, to see, to remember

I giggle
she shines
her smile warms me, I bask
her eyes tell me, I know
her arms embrace me—I am safe

## DONNA PINTER

I'm here

I exhale, slowly, with intention

I remember

I open my eyes, to see

# Colouring

After you died we could not (perhaps would not) use
dark pens of any kind because they felt inked
with the same-skinned bruise that spread
and spread its way to pages soiled and stalled.

Even the garden violets—small contusions—planted
only with your name in mind seemed so
untouchably and unreachably blue.

Some botanical pendants might strictly argue purple,
but no matter about splitting the palate here—
For the sake of those who wish to paint
or write you into view, let us simply say

*flowers.*

## Sweet Peas

*for my parents*

*The green shoot will break through the rock . . . our tombs of loss will shatter, and there will be a Homecoming. There will. There will. There will.*

*Lewis Packer*

Every year your hands wire trellis to the sloping fence
staking out the hope of something more than grey.

Then with a watering can you form a nimbus cloud
and rain on seeds in drought-bound soil.

We wait not knowing when the awkward stalk who keeps
tight-lipped for weeks might have something to say.

And always, every year, the first flower calls us outside
to hear its perfumed mouth finally speak colour.

## The Superhero

Good, evil
Hero, villain
Evil, good?

The difference.
Is there a difference?
We're told to believe
in concepts
arbitrary, greater
than ourselves.

Greater than what?

So persuaded,
we won't see.
That the fairytale
isn't
in concepts, arbitrary.

Good, evil.
Hero, villain.
It's in us.

Isn't it?

# Currawong's End

She came wobbling out of the sky and landed at my feet. I was stunned that she could still fly. There was an empty socket where her eye used to be. It oozed a jellied bloodied mess. The lower half of her beak was detached from her pounded skull. Lacerations criss crossed her twisted form and warm blood dripped down her body and pooled at the end of her claws. Every breath was a laboured struggle for a moment more of precious life.

She gobbled down the mince I gave her and then painfully gathered as much as a broken beak could bear and flew away in her awkward wobbly way. I knew then, that there were squawking baby birds over in the line of gums, whose lives depended on her ability to provide food for them. Day after day, morning and night, she came.

Day after day, morning and night, I fed her. The wounds slowly healed and she started to gain some strength. I was so happily relieved. Death had crept out of the night slipping his scythe gently around her neck dragging her slowly into his shadow. But we had fought him off. I truly thought that we had won.

For a few months she did so well. I was awed by the sheer courage and determination that brought a bunch of squabbling balls of black feathered fun onto the deck one morning. What a joyous day. But the joy was short lived. It marked the turning point. Her life's song began to fade into death's dark night.

She grew weaker and weaker until she could barely move. She came and sat at my feet with her head on her chest, striking the pose of her final rest. There was no more fight in her. I picked her up without a struggle and held her against me, gently stroking those crumpled feathers. The pain filled hours passing by as I watched her slowly die.

I loved her. I weep as though she was a family member lost– for she was.

I mourn for her– I mourn for us who struggle and fight for life, and think we've won.

## Lake Life

Fingers of the wind whisper
through the spindly She Oaks
that are bending and stretching before
its gentle caress.

I sway in time with the haunting raspy whistle
Spray splashes on my skin
Leaving its cooling crust of salt to remind me
that all is right in this child's world.

A rickety cottage perched precariously on the edge
of Lake Macquarie, leans reassuringly into my back.
The sun is squatting low in the brightly orange western sky,
And the shadows start to gallop across the patches of grass
we call yard.

A ride weary Dragster lays where it was thrust
Into the ground at the end of its usefulness,
Rubber encrusted spinning spokes of
the green fun machine
now turning lazily in the air.

Peeling red velvet baroque wallpaper
And cracked tired and flaking old paint.
Welcome warmth of a poor man's castle,
Crumbling asbestos of joy.

## A Horse, A House, A Girl

Bright blue eyes, pixie blonde hair
almost the same size, but she beat me there
In that dilapidated house decades older than me
was a stable, riding trails and the grandest climbing tree

Our horses carried us across the yard,
ducking under the washing line and
soaring above the overgrown stump,
galloping until our little legs gave way

If she was feeling brave she would lead us
to that eerie, secret hideaway that was mysterious
Leaving our horses behind we would crawl
into the clearing with all of the rubble

A rusted high chair and an old bike tyre
Oh! the wonderful treasures we'd find there
in that sanctuary where we'd hide from the neighbour
and transport ourselves into another realm

As the sun disappeared and our mother came calling
we'd retrace the steps that we'd taken that morning
Sit down to dinner and eat so we were ready
to go galloping again after school the next evening

Over time the stables vanished and the riding trails faded
until all that remained were overgrown shrubs that were jaded
Leading by example my sister began
to shower instead of bath and comb her own hair

Forced to move house, they knocked it all down
the stables, the hideaway; our imaginary town
We traded our horses for clothes and jewellery
and chased after boys instead of each other

# Bookworm

Eyes strain against the dark,
the glow of the lamp only just bright enough
to separate words from page

"Be different and be damned";
"Hardships make or break people"
And yet
"Tomorrow is another day"

Tears fill her big hazel eyes,
threatening to spill over cracked porcelain cheeks
The flames of the fire and long-haired tabby
are all that keep her withering frame company

Rolling green hills and white painted fences,
tattered relationships scattered 'round town
Face aglow and hand unsteady
her vision of Clayton County is fading

Whole body shaking she rises from her rocker;
the grey ball of fluff follows.
On the stained chestnut coffee table
the well-thumbed novel remains

*Be different and be damned*

# ASHLEY STEELE

She primps her greying black hair
*Hardships make or break people*
She curls up in bed, alone
*Tomorrow is another day*
She can barely picture his face anymore

Sun streaks in through moth eaten curtains;
dust and cat hair fill the air
She pulls her frail body out from the sheets
and stands before the mirror

Though she has never seen Scarlett O'Hara
Scarlett is staring straight back at her
Dull hazel eyes, wispy peppered hair
and like Scarlett she longs for him

# Coin of My Life

Coin of my life, what is your story? Worth a quarter dollar yet invaluable, your sides smooth from a lifetime of use. Who possessed you? The inconvenient change weighing down the pocket of a businessman, thrown to a homeless beggar, to whom you were his all. What have you purchased? Were you lost amongst countless others fed into a vending machine for a can of Coca-Cola, or were you the precious savings of a child, placed carefully into his piggy bank – twenty-five cents closer to his dream toy. Were you flipped to make decisions? The ringing sound as you were propelled skyward, all eyes on you as you spun into the air. You chime on impact with the ground, the quickening metallic reverberations, like the shimmering of a cymbal. As your fast spins turn to slower wobbles, the intensity around you rises. In this moment, you hold all power: which outcome will you reveal? Were you ever used to make a wish? Young couple's fingers entwine as they trace your path from their hands to the pool that lay before them. Sinking below the surface, the only hint of your existence: the ripples left behind, and the memory shared between two lovers. As you join other coins that were sealed with a kiss in hope for a happily ever after, you wonder if their wish ever did come true.

Coin of my life, you chose me. Together we have shared many more memories, as you hang from my neck, close to my heart. "E Pluribus Unum", boldly written above the eagle on your front: "out of many, one". Coin of *my* life; I am but a *part* of yours.

## Your Garden

*for Roley*

Your garden,
where the fairies dwell
an enchanted forest you grew
with your old, weary hands
creased with dirt
for the one you love.

There lay your bonsais; a miniature Eden
contorted trunks
from which fairies would peek
like I, the heart of your devotion
like I, a treasure growing.

Across the damp stone bridge
I watch the fairies spring
skipping the stepping stones
hugged by moss

Every night, to the lantern, to the ball
every night, your footsteps behind me
placing my small feet on your own,
balancing, we lock, we twirl,
we waltz

In your garden, mine –
Ours.

# Fieldwork

The hilltop backs onto a concrete hedge,
urban towers that are sheltered
by a stand of trees: native gums,
strewn figs and a pair of hoop pines, older
than the root-broken tar-gravel path below.

As much an enclosure as an open field,
this slope is home to the red-blue winged
swallow, the white moth, the lapwing
and the crow. Home to earth-digging
corellas, the pestilent myna and its pesky herd.

And one day to a magpie who,
bedraggled, lay face down on the path.
I first thought it a crow until, angling it up
with my boot, I saw her grey upper tail,
her white rump and ashy underwing.

A gassy stench rose from under her
and field ants moved in and out of her beak.
With two thickish twigs, I stretchered her
over to the foot of a pine, buried her
with matted conifer brush, debris and leaves.

I left her there to the hide beetles
and the flesh-boring burying beetles,
who would come to grapple through seed-cone,
stick and leaf, mud, and at last, by way
of orifice, would sheath her, nosh on her

ripe tissue and fleshy muck, before leaving
eggs in a crypt scraped under her remains.
Larvae would move into beetledom, into
the birthwing of the hutted carcass, and there
draw on the phlegmy gush of blood and bone.

Later, when I saw that the wind had threshed
the burial to a thatch of knotted sticks,
I eagerly peered into an opening, rummaged
through empty afterwork to find clumped
feathers and a wing, partially intact.

Digging further, I hit upon a skull,
then another. The first, that of a petite bird,
a swallow perhaps – its vertebrae
like the cast mould of an unset jewel.
The second was clearly that of the magpie.

I stepped back and stood staring
into the hollowed-out eyes, the gone brain,
spiralling and turning it upside down,
prying the underside with my eye, thumbing
and spinning it into a circle, thinking,

and even speaking: I know what the cycle
serves, but what is being served by
the cycle? It's arguable, I know – best
to just walk and fall in love with the field,
the beloved range of the ubiquitous grass.

TODD TURNER

## Guinea Fowl

With a quail-shaped body
and a vulture-like head
they look like crossbred turkeys
or blue-ribbon hybrid hens.
Though in the kingdom of birds
this seemingly assorted
mixed bag is an independent flock
who, in slate-dark plumage
and moony-bright spots,
quills that a milliner would crave,
scratch around like Miss Marple,
stealthy as barnyard cats.
Nimble-footed in stifling
frocks, shrewd and antisocial,
they scour the land like ducks on water
but are nowhere near as quaint.
And they're far too busy
to swan about in a peacock suit
with the air of a lark ascending.
Theirs is the head down
hard-nosed blitz of unruly order,
driven as if by recompense or dutiful need.
In a gregarious grey-cloud tumbleweed
tight-knit pack, they've come to rid
the paddocks of seasonal peril:
locusts, spiders, ticks

and old bald-faced misery.
Together they're in their element,
relentlessly rummaging,
constantly bending and pecking,
rooted to the spot at hand
in fastidious delight.
They do not care for the manacles
of a bygone world: kingdoms
of a fallen age, empires in the dust.
It's the sovereign dirt beneath their feet
and the babble of whistling chirps,
the workaday nod and lancing of beaks
that sets them apart from the hunt
in the grass.
                    As for the snake—
out from its pit of a hollowed log,
uncoiled as the rays of the sun,
needling through the underbrush
like a thick plait rivering in swards of green,
craving, I suppose, to slither head-on
into the banquet on the henhouse floor—
morning has lured it out in the open,
freed it from the nocturnal swoop
of an owl and the hunt of a ravenous fox.
And as dawn unfurls in swathes
of random order, cold-blooded
with earthly hunger the snake
slides-on, red tongue hissing,

a slick of fire across the feral sprawl.
Though in the eye of the guineas
it's merely a link in the chain of pests.
They'll spot one wriggling
in the burning distance or coldly
stalking under hot-flushed straw.
Then one by one they band together,
surround it in encircling ranks,
and with machinery screeches
they scourge in a cross-fire attack,
butchering it from head to tail
until the snake lies twitching
like a severed limb. And through
the punctured scales of its deathly skin,
in holes where there once were eyes,
they riddle it over with jackhammering pecks
leaving nothing more than a plaything,
bones for the driveling wind.

## Nana's Seashells

The salty Spring air
Kisses her lips,
Soft eyes seeking treasure —
Creased hands search
The sanative sand,
As the sweetness of her smile
Grows stronger.

Seashells, glass and
Bottle caps
Suffuse her satin purse —
As her infant spirit
Is swept aloft,
She dances effervescently
In the salvific breeze.

Her mind sailing
Out to sea,
Baptised in ocean spray —
As sapient waves
Crash to shore,
Silently whispering, "hush"

I hold her seashells.

# ALEESHA WHATSON

## Rain

Encapsulated in white briefcases
life is transported
gliding effortlessly across
continents I've never visited

Hurried by the wind —
Earth's sacred breath —
they grow as hot air balloons
or scared puffer fish.

A cloak of darkness
ensnares the sun;
the sky's piercing screams
signify the battle's been won.

Buckles burst open
as the Earth yields her prize,
the briefcases emptied
landing on my windowsill alongside

my thoughts.

The sun rebukes darkness' grasp
as the rain and thunder ceases.
My thoughts soon to ascend once more
to be transported in white briefcases.

# Editors' Notes

*'... into thanks, and silence in which*
*another voice may speak ... .'*
— Mary Oliver, 'Thirst'

We offer colossal thanks again to Dr David Musgrave from Puncher and Wattmann who has been instrumental in the publication of this anthology. Appreciation and thanks goes to the Avondale College of Higher Education creative writing class for their enthusiasm and commitment in developing their work for this anthology; it has been a joy and inspiration working with them.

An enormous measure of gratitude is offered here to the established poets who generously contributed their voices and work to this year's anthology, and in so doing have enriched the quality and breadth of poetry on offer.

The cover design for this anthology represents the professional process Donna Pinter engages in with her Avondale students from the 'That Design' studio, and we thank each of them for participating in the client briefing process. In particular, we acknowledge Chloe Lwin for her innovative cover design. We are also grateful for David Page's creative and managerial skills in overseeing the graphic design collateral for the project, and his impeccable work. We also deeply value the input into the anthology design from Puncher and Wattmann's Matthew Holt.

For her generous and expert assistance with the preparation of the anthology manuscript, we pay tribute to Margaret House. For support with the book launch event and catering we thank Nick Hartigan and his team. We also take this opportunity to thank the financial services department at Avondale for their assistance, and especially note Paul Hattingh's significant contribution to the College.

In showcasing the launch of *All These Presences*, we recognise again Professor Jane Fernandez, Professor Anthony Williams and Professor Ray Roennfeldt for their ongoing support. We express our appreciation for Associate Professor Paul Race, Dean of the Faculty of Arts, Nursing and Theology, for valuing this project and the efforts of those involved, along with Associate Professor Maria Northcote's vision for pedagogical innovation in her role as director of the Centre for Advancement of the Scholarship of Teaching and Learning.

And to our inspired colleagues working in the Arts, and the many well-wishers who have passed on their encouragement for publishing this anthology, your support of and engagement with poetry remains paramount.

—Jean Kent, David Musgrave and Carolyn Rickett

July 2016

# Biographies

HAYLEY ANTOLOS is studying film and television at Deakin University in Melbourne, and has found writing to be an invaluable means of expression, healing and creativity. Her love of the arts extends from filmmaking and songwriting, to screenplays and poetry. Currently, Hayley is expanding her love of poetry whilst working on a novel.

KYLE ARMSTRONG was born in Brisbane and has spent most of his years in rural Queensland. His interests include pottery, coffee and when it can be afforded, travel. Kyle is currently completing a Bachelor of Arts (Communication Major) at Avondale College of Higher Education.

LYN BARDEN is a Senior English teacher at Barker College in Sydney. Teaching has taken her far and wide; from Newcastle, Raymond Terrace, The Entrance and Teacher Education at Macquarie University. Poetry is her "quiet passion". Lyn champions journal writing with her students and encourages poetic inclusions to stimulate the imagination.

JUDITH BEVERIDGE is the author of six books of poetry. She is currently working on her *New and Selected Poems* to be published by Giramondo in 2017. She teaches poetry at postgraduate level at The University of Sydney.

PETER BOYLE has published six collections of poetry, including *Towns in the Great Desert* (2013) and *Apocrypha* (2009). A new book *Ghostspeaking* is due out this year. He also translates poetry from French and Spanish and is currently completing a Doctorate of Creative Arts at Western Sydney University.

ALLY BURSTON is a third year university student from Ellalong, New South Wales. She is currently studying a degree in Secondary Education with a major in Modern History and a minor in English. Ally unashamedly enjoys adolescent dystopian and post-apocalyptic fiction whilst also relishing the romance of Jane Austen. She has never been one to write poetry, but has savoured this opportunity to combine her love of stories and ballroom dancing.

MICHELLE CAHILL writes poetry, essays and fiction. *The Herring Lass* is forthcoming with Arc; *Letter to Pessoa* (Giramondo) is a collection of prize-winning short fiction. She is editor of the online literary magazine *Mascara* and co-editor of the anthology *Contemporary Asian Australian Poets.*

EILEEN CHONG is a Sydney poet who was born in Singapore. Her books are *Burning Rice* (2012), *Peony* (2014) and *Painting Red Orchids* (2016), all from Pitt Street Poetry. Her work has been shortlisted for multiple awards, including the Prime Minister›s Literary Award and the Anne Elder Award. In 2016 she started Potts Point Press which issues limited edition letterpressed Australian poetry. www.eileenchong.com.au

WILLIAM CHRISTIE After 35 years teaching in the Department of English at University of Sydney, William Christie moved to the Australian National University where he is Head of its Humanities Research Centre. Past President of the Romantic Studies Association of Australasia (RSAA), he is Fellow and Head of the English Section at the Australian Academy of the Humanities. His scholarly publications include *Samuel Taylor Coleridge: A Literary Life* (2006) – awarded the NSW Premier's Biennial Prize for Literary Scholarship in 2008 – *The Edinburgh Review in the Literary Culture of Romantic Britain* (2009), *Dylan Thomas: A Literary Life* (2014), and *The Two Romanticisms, and Other Essays* (2016). For many years president of the Dylan Thomas Society of Australia and an active member of a number of literary societies, William Christie is also the author of *Under Mulga Wood* (2004), an award-winning play for voices that has enjoyed performances around the country and been broadcast and recorded by the ABC.

KERRYN COOMBS-VALEONTIS is an art and horticultural therapist working in mental health, and a TAFE teacher. She is studying poetry therapy through the International Poetry Therapy Academy, and begins to agree with Gregory Orr: that poetry is survival. Her first poem was published in Western Sydney's *ZineWest* in 2015.

JORDAN COSTIGAN is a fourth year student studying a Bachelor of Arts, specialising in communication. Ironically, Jordan avoided English and writing classes throughout his life, however, after taking a communication unit in his third year of university, he discovered he had a natural creativity and way with words. This sparked a new love for writing, and he is now striving to build a career in the field of communication. Jordan's dream job would be to write poetry and short stories full time.

LUCY DOUGAN'S books include *Meanderthals* (Web del Sol), *White Clay* and *The Guardians* (Giramondo). She works for the magazines *Westerly* and *Axon*, and teaches in the creative writing programme at Curtin University.

STEPHEN EDGAR is the author of ten collections of poetry, the most recent being *Exhibits of the Sun* (Black Pepper, 2014). In 2012 *The Red Sea: New and Selected Poems* (Baskerville) was published in the US. His website is stephenedgar.com.au.

BROOK EMERY'S most recent book, *Collusion*, was shortlisted for the Western Australian Premier's Literary Awards. His previous three books were all short-listed for the Kenneth Slessor Prize. *and dug my fingers in the sand* won the Judith Wright Calanthe Prize.

JANE FERNANDEZ is Vice-President (Quality & Strategy) at *Avondale College of Higher Education*. Jane is also founding convenor of the *Higher Education Private Provider Quality Network* (HEPP-QN). Jane's interest is in leadership in higher education quality and practice. Jane is committed to developing and extending the quality foot-print of private higher education nationally in Australia and develops and leads quality projects to support this vision. Her academic background is in postcolonial literature. Her research interests include institutional quality assurance as well as postcolonial literary criticism.

JOHN FOULCHER'S tenth book of poetry, a collection from his previous volumes is *101 Poems* (Pitt St Poetry 2015). He lives in Canberra.

ANITA GERSBACH was born in Auckland, New Zealand, but quickly whisked away to be raised by a beach near Newcastle, Australia. She has a passion for nature (specifically the ocean) and being immersed in the natural world. And sometimes she dabbles in writing.

ALTHEA HALLIDAY is a Senior English teacher at Barker College in Sydney. Throughout her career she has encouraged her students to celebrate creativity and embrace the power of words. In recent times, she has discovered Dylan Thomas' *Under Milk Wood* and has taken as her mantra Thomas' exhortation to the readers of his radio play in 1953, 'Love the words.'

CLAUDIA HOUSTOUN grew up in a variety of rural towns and now lives in Toowoomba, Queensland. She edits the Avondale College student magazine, *The Voice*, and is studying to be a secondary English and Studies of Religion teacher.

JASMINE HUNTER was born and grew up in Perth, Western Australia. She is currently studying a Bachelor of Arts at Avondale College of Higher Education. Majoring in International Development and Poverty Studies, she hopes to work internationally for a non-government organisation upon graduation. Communication is her second major, which will be of great use to her when advocating about different worldly injustices she may come across in her future work.

SOPHIA HUSBAND is an avid reader and lover of words. She is enchanted by prose and poetry which explores the connections between family, history, memory and spirituality. When she is unleashed to teach future generations she hopes to instil in her students a passion for the arts.

DANIEL IONITA Born in Bucharest, Romania, Daniel teaches Organisational Improvement at the University of Technology Sydney. Published works include *Testament – Anthology of Modern Romanian Verse*, the first comprehensive collection of Romanian poetry in English, and a couple of volumes of his own poems *Hanging Between the Stars* and *Contra Diction.*

LINDA IRELAND has had work published in several Hunter anthologies, including *A Slow Combusting Hymn* (ASM and Cerberus Press, 2014). In 2016 she was invited to be a Community Teaching Assistant with Modpo, an international online course on modern American poetry developed through the University of Pennsylvania. A member of Blue Room Poets, Linda has helped establish Poetry in the Pub in Western Lake Macquarie.

CAROL JENKINS has two books published: *Fishing in the Devonian* (2008) shortlisted for the Victorian Premiers and Ann Elder Awards and *Xn* (2013) shortlisted for the WA Premiers Award. Both are published by Puncher & Wattmann, who will also publish her next book S*elect Episodes from The Mr Farmhand Series* in 2016. She blogs at Show Me the Treasure, and established River Road Press to record and publish Australian poets reading their own work.

SARAH JENKINS is a student studying secondary teaching at Avondale College. She runs *The Real Sisters Leto*, an online blog that welcomes reader's contributions, and is an avid TV show watcher – the root of all her inspiration.

JUDY JOHNSON has published five full length poetry collections. Her prizes include The Victorian Premier's Award, The Josephine Ulrick and Val Vallis Awards. Her most recent collection *Stone Scar Air Water* was shortlisted in the West Australian Premier's Awards, and a selection of the poems won the Wesley Michel Wright Prize, an award she also won in 2004 with a selection from *Nomadic*.

SUE JOSEPH has been a journalist for more than thirty-five years, working in Australia and the UK. She began working as an academic, teaching print journalism at the University of Technology Sydney in 1997. As a Senior Lecturer, she now teaches and supervises journalism and creative writing, particularly creative non-fiction writing, in both undergraduate and postgraduate programs. Her research interests are around sexuality, secrets and confession, framed by the media; HIV and women; ethics; trauma; supervision and ethics and life writing; and Australian creative non-fiction. She is the author of *Speaking Secrets* (2012, Alto Books) and *Behind the Text: Candid conversations with Australian creative nonfiction writers* (2016, Hybrid Publishers).

CHRISTOPHER (KIT) KELEN is a well-known Australian poet, scholar and visual artist, and Professor of English at the University of Macau, where he has taught Creative Writing and Literature for the last sixteen years. The most recent of Kit Kelen's dozen English language poetry books is *Scavengers Season*, published by Puncher and Wattman in 2014. Kit Kelen is the Editor of the new cross-arts international on-line journal *the wonderbook* and is Literary Editor for *Postcolonial Text*. In 2016 he is co-ordinating Project 366, a daily on-line collaboration of poets and artists.

JEAN KENT grew up in rural Queensland and now lives at Lake Macquarie. She has published five full-length poetry collections. Her most recent books are *The Hour of Silvered Mullet* (Pitt Street Poetry, 2015) and *Paris in my Pocket* (PSP, 2016), a selection of her poems from an Australia Council residency in Paris. With Kit Kelen, in 2014

Jean co-edited *A Slow Combusting Hymn: Poetry from and about Newcastle and the Hunter Region.*

ANGELINA KERR is a final year Bachelor of Arts student at Avondale College of Higher Education. With a passion for travelling to new places, she is majoring in International Poverty and Development and hopes to be a successful adult in the future. In her spare time she also enjoys reading and music and considers herself to be an avid connoisseur of vegetarian food. Working for an overseas NGO is her ultimate dream, which she will pursue more seriously after graduation.

ANDY KISSANE lives in Bardwell Park and writes poetry and fiction. His books include his fourth collection of poetry, *Radianc*e (Puncher & Wattmann, 2014), which was shortlisted for the 2015 Victorian Premier's Prize for Poetry, *Out to Lunch*, and a book of short stories, *The Swarm.* http://andykissane.com

SHARNA KOSMEIER grew up in various towns in New Zealand and NSW Australia. She is in her second year of studying a Bachelor of Arts, specialising in Communication and minoring in Marketing. Two tasks that clear her head are running and writing, however she has an immense appreciation for other people's attempts at the latter, especially if satirical.

RICHARD LANDER is retired and commenced writing poetry as a form of therapy after being diagnosed with prostate cancer in 2007. He is married to Lyndall and lives in Sydney. Some of Richard's other poetry has been published in *The New Leaves Poetry Anthology*, *Wording the World*, and *Here not there*.

MARTIN LANGFORD has published seven books of poetry, the most recent of which is *Ground* (P&W, 2015). He is the editor of *Harbour City Poems: Sydney in Verse 1788-2008* (P&W, 2009). He has directed three Australian Poetry Festivals, and is the Deputy Chair of Australian Poetry Ltd. He is the poetry reviewer for *Meanjin.*

LYNNETTE LOUNSBURY is a lecturer in Communication and Ancient History, and a creative arts practitioner at Avondale College. She is the author of the young adult novel *Afterworld* (Allen & Unwin, 2014) and her second novel *We ate the Road like Vultures* (Inkerman & Blunt) was published in April 2016.

GREG McLAREN is a Sydney-based poet, critic and teacher. His books include *The Kurri Kurri Book of the Dead* (Puncher & Wattmann, 2007) and *After Han Shan* (Flying Islands, 2012). He has been anthologised in *Windchimes: Asia in Australian Poetry* (Eds: Noel Rowe and Vivian Smith), *Australian Poetry since 1788* (Eds: Robert Gray and Geoffrey Lehmann) and in *Contemporary Australian Poetry* (Eds: Judith Beveridge, David Musgrave, Martin Langford and Judy Johnson). A new book, *Australian ravens*, was published by Puncher & Wattmann this year.

LAURA MITCHELL grew up in Sydney when housing prices were affordable and has a genuine love for anything covered in polka dots. As a lover of words and performing, Laura hopes to pursue a career in radio. Her two goals in life are to star in a musical and to run through a field of giant sunflowers.

TAFLIN MOWBRAY was born, grown, and is still yet to be kicked out of, her home town of Lismore, NSW. She is a student of Communications and History at Avondale and has a passion for art and debating philosophy. She hopes one day to publish some of the endless stories that crowd her head, and to live in a library.

VIEMA MURRAY credits her parents' bedtime stories with her passion for creative writing. In fact, her love for the written word is what led her to pursue a career as an English teacher. Apart from reading and writing, Viema enjoys exploring, drawing and singing along animatedly to musicals. She is currently in in her final year studying a Bachelor of Arts/Bachelor of Teaching at Avondale College of Higher Education.

DAVID MUSGRAVE is the author of the novel, *Glissando: a Melodrama*. His latest collection of poetry is *Concrete Tuesday*, Island Press 2011. He runs the publishing company Puncher and Wattmann and lectures in creative writing at the University of Newcastle. He has won numerous awards for his poetry.

MARCEL NEUHOFF was born in Bethlehem, South Africa, but grew up in Adelaide, and currently lives with friends in Cooranbong, NSW. A lover of letters and past wisdom, he will complete a Bachelor Arts through Avondale College later this year, with majors in English and History. In his spare moments from study, he likes to travel and read as frequently as possible.

JAN OWEN is a South Australian poet and translator who has published six books of verse. A volume of new and selected poems, *The Offhand Angel*, was published in London by Eyewear Publishing in 2015 and her volume of translations from Baudelaire's *Les Fleurs du Mal* was published in the same year by Arc Publications.

DONNA PINTER is a designer, educator, fashion enthusiast, amateur poet, wife to Dean and mother of two beautiful girls … Ruby and Coco. In addition to owning a boutique graphic design firm, satellite ink, Donna lectures in graphic design and manages Avondale's student graphic design studio 'That Design'. Donna is creatively pursuing her heart's path by fearlessly making marks with design, typography, colour, conversation, paint, photography and the written word. For her, within this mix, poetry is a tonic.

CAROLYN RICKETT is an Assistant Dean (Research), a Senior Lecturer in Communication and creative arts practitioner at Avondale College of Higher Education. She is co-ordinator for *The New Leaves* writing project, an initiative for people who have experienced or are experiencing the trauma of a life-threatening illness. Together with Judith Beveridge, she is co-editor of *The New Leaves Poetry Anthology*. Other poetry anthologies she has co-edited with Judith include: *Wording the World*, *Here not there* and *A Way of Happening*. Her research interests cover autobiographical writing as a therapeutic intervention, cancer narratives, trauma studies, poetry praxis and journalism practice. She is currently working on a narrative nonfiction book of travel stories.

ZOE ROMERO HILTON was raised in sunny Queensland where her mother instilled in her a love of words which continues to this day. This love prompted Zoe to pursue a career in communications where she hopes to make writing her full-time job. When she's not reading or writing, Zoe can be found pursuing a film hobby with her husband.

TANIA ROSSITER is an environmental activist, running a project called Kelpie's Clean Up, helping to raise awareness on the issue of plastic in the oceans. She is a photographer and underwater videographer, recently winning a number of awards in short film festivals. In her spare time she is studying a Bachelor of Arts at Avondale College with a major in Counselling and minor in Communication.

ASHLEY STEELE began writing for leisure as a child when, bored at her mum's work, she was pushed to find something to entertain her mind. After falling victim to the travel bug at the age of 14, she went on to volunteer in Cambodia for two months in 2014. Now studying a Bachelor of Arts, specialising in Communication and majoring in International Poverty and Development Studies, she longs to combine her passion for travel and writing by working for an NGO to help others.

ISABELLA STRATFORD enjoys the company of her dogs over that of most humans and is never opposed to taking a nap (with her dogs). She excels at talking too much, spending her savings on travel, and giving quality hugs. Her love of words, particularly those of Sylvia Plath, has found her in her third year of a Bachelor of Arts/Bachelor of Teaching degree, and she hopes to one day further her education in the field of Counselling.

TODD TURNER'S first collection of poetry *Woodsmoke* was published by Black Pepper Publishing. His poems have been published in journals, newspapers and anthologies. He has been shortlisted in the Blake and Newcastle Poetry Prize and in 2013 he was the joint-winner of the inaugural Jean Cecily Drake-Brockman Poetry Prize.

ALEESHA WHATSON resides along the beautiful Lake Macquarie with her seven fish, two cats, two dogs and 8-year-old rabbit named Twinkle. A lover of sunsets and adventure, she enjoys keeping active and finds great joy in wordplay, much to her friends' annoyance. Majoring in English, Aleesha has immense passion for youth, and is excited to commence her teaching career.

## Acknowledgements

Judith Beveridge's 'Herons at Dusk' is from *Storm and Honey*, Giramondo Publishing, 2009; 'Naming Roses' is from *Accidental Grace*, UQP, 1996.

Peter Boyle's 'Conversation while waiting' was first published (in an earlier version) in *Southerly*.

Eileen Chong's 'Secrets' is from *Painting Red Orchids*, Pitt Street Poetry, 2016.

Lucy Dougan's 'The Shy Dog' and 'Julia, Reading' are from *The Guardians*, Giramondo Publishing, 2016.

Stephen Edgar's 'Jupiter' was previously published in *The Weekend Australian Review*.

Brook Emery's 'must' was first published in the *Canberra Times*. 'The right time to write' was published in the *Australian Poetry Journal*.

John Foulcher's 'Ash' was originally published in *Quadrant*, April 2015.

Linda Ireland's 'Exotic' and 'Codes to Leave' were first published in *Grieve* 2016 (Hunter Writers Centre).

Carol Jenkins' 'Night gardening, mauve and mutable' was first published in *Snorkel* #20, December 2014.

Judy Johnson's 'St Kevin and the Blackbird' is from *Stone Scar Air Water*, Walleah Press, 2013; 'Photography at Dingo Creek' is from *Nomadic*, Black Pepper Press, 2004.

Kit Kelen's 'to tend' and 'advice for poets' are from *a pocket kit 2*, Flying Island Books, 2016.

Jean Kent's 'A Night Without Curtains' is from *Practising Breathing*, Hale & Iremonger, 1991; 'Translating a Prolog' is from *The Language of Light*, Flying Island Books, 2013.

Andy Kissane's 'Beached Dreams' was published in *Peace, Tolerance & Understanding: Poems from the ACU Poetry Prize*, Australian Catholic University, 2015. 'Waiting Beside You' was published in *Grieve 2015*, Hunter Writers Centre, 2015.

Martin Langford's 'The Beach' is from *Faultlines* (Round Table,

1991); 'Silence of Frogs' is from *The Human Project* (Puncher & Wattmann, 2009).

Greg McLaren's 'Teralba' and 'South Maitland' are from *Australian Ravens*, Puncher & Wattmann, 2016.

Jan Owen's 'A Little Wine' was published in *The Offhand Angel*, Eyewear, London, 2015; 'Anticipation' was published in *Cordite 52: Toil.*

Carolyn Rickett's 'Sweet Peas' and 'Colouring' are from *A Slow Combusting Hymn: Poetry from and about Newcastle and the Hunter Region*, (Eds) Kit Kelen and Jean Kent, Australia, ASM and Cerberus Press, 2014.

Todd Turner's 'Fieldwork' was published in his first collection, *Woodsmoke*, Black Pepper Publishing, 2014. It also appeared in the *Australian Poetry Journal*, Volume 1 no. 1, 2011. 'Guinea Fowl' was shortlisted for the 2015 Newcastle Poetry Prize and published in the prize anthology, *Connective Tissue* (Hunter Writers Centre, 2015).

www.ingramcontent.com/pod-product-compliance
Lightning Source LLC
Chambersburg PA
CBHW030831090426
42737CB00009B/971
*9781922186928*